The Saga of Pistol Pete

The Saga of Pistol Pete

Doug Hensley

Ingram spark

CONTENTS

The Legend Of Pistol Pete
By
Doug Hensley
Table Of Contents

Chapter 1: The Trail Begins

- Introduction to Pistol Pete and the mysterious stranger
- Pete's life as a scout and his encounter with the stranger
- Mysterious events hinting at the untamed frontier

Chapter 2: Shadows of the Mesquite Grove

- Pete and the stranger explore the mystical mesquite grove
- Encounter with ancient spirits and tales of the grove
- Unveiling the stranger's enigmatic past

Chapter 3: Veins of the Silver Canyon

- Journey into the heart of the Silver Canyon
- Discovery of silver-hued stone and hidden alcoves
- Encounters with frontier challenges and adversaries

Chapter 4: Whispers of the Mystic Oasis

- Arrival at the legendary Mystic Oasis

- Exploration of the enchanted waters and surrounding meadows
- Uncovering the oasis's mystical history

Chapter 5: Dance of the Prairie Spirits

- Riding through vast prairies and discovering sacred stone circles
- Connection to the prairie spirits and their untold stories
- Pete's growing awareness of his role in the frontier's tapestry

Chapter 6: Secrets of the Whispering Pines

- Trekking through dense pine forests
- Encounters with mysterious figures and creatures
- Whispering pines revealing ancient secrets

Chapter 7: Echoes in the Caverns of Time

- Delving into mysterious caverns
- Discovery of ancient cave paintings and artifacts
- Time-traveling elements revealing the untamed past

Chapter 8: Storm on the Horizon

- Dark clouds gather as a storm approaches
- Challenges intensify, testing Pete and the stranger
- Unraveling of personal histories amid adversity

Chapter 9: The Sentinel Peaks

- Ascending towering peaks to gain a vantage point
- Observing the vastness of the frontier
- Revelations about the journey and its purpose

Chapter 10: Enchantment of the Moonlit Marsh

- Navigating through a surreal marsh under the moonlight
- Encounter with mystical creatures and guardian spirits
- Pete and the stranger confronting inner fears

Chapter 11: Fireside Tales and Revelations

- Campfire discussions revealing deeper truths
- Sharing personal stories and motives
- Strengthening the bond between Pete and the stranger

Chapter 12: Spirits of the Forgotten Ghost Town

- Stumbling upon a ghost town with a haunted history
- Interactions with lingering spirits
- Confrontations with the unresolved past

Chapter 13: Shadows Across the Sand Dunes

- Crossing expansive sand dunes under the scorching sun
- Mirage-like encounters and illusions
- Pete's resilience and determination tested

Chapter 14: Celestial Harmony in the Starlit Sky

- Nights spent under the vast celestial dome
- Reflections on the interconnectedness of the universe
- Pete and the stranger seeking guidance from the stars

Chapter 15: Serenade of the Waterfall

- Discovering a majestic waterfall hidden within the wilderness

- Renewal and cleansing amid the cascading waters
- The waterfall as a symbol of hope and rebirth

Chapter 16: Labyrinth of the Enchanted Lagoon

- Navigating through a labyrinthine lagoon surrounded by bio-luminescent flora
- Encounter with mystical creatures and ancient guardians
- The lagoon as a passage to the next phase of the journey

17: Guardians of the Forgotten Temple

- Stumbling upon a forgotten temple in the heart of the frontier
- Confronting guardians and deciphering ancient rites
- Pete and the stranger's roles in the temple's mystery

Chapter 18: The Eldritch Winds

- Journey through a desolate landscape marked by eerie winds
- Encounter with eldritch forces and ethereal entities
- Unraveling the connection between Pete and the stranger

Chapter 19: Echoes of the Final Confrontation

- Gathering storm as Pete and the stranger face ultimate challenges
- Showdown with adversaries from the past
- Revelations leading to the climax of the journey

Chapter 20: The Unending Frontier

- Resolution and aftermath of the journey
- Pete and the stranger part ways, each carrying the lessons of the frontier

- Closing the chapter on the untamed wilderness, leaving it forever imprinted on their souls.

Author's Notes

In the heart of the untamed Wild West, where the dust of the frontier conceals secrets as ancient as the land itself, emerges a legendary figure known only as "Pistol Pete." In "Pistol Pete's Odyssey," embark on a gripping journey that transcends the boundaries of folklore, weaving together supernatural encounters, temporal anomalies, and clandestine conspiracies that shape the destiny of a frontier town.

As mysterious forces stir beneath the starlit skies, "Pistol Pete" becomes the town's vigilant guardian, confronting a host of enigmatic adversaries that defy mortal comprehension. From a bone-chilling encounter with the ancient Wendigo to navigating the delicate balance between celestial anomalies and temporal rifts, the legendary figure faces challenges that test not only his marksmanship but the very fabric of reality.

The narrative unfolds with a spectral lament that echoes through the Wild West, leading "Pistol Pete" on a journey through forgotten legacies and ethereal realms. As the haunting strains reveal untold stories and unresolved conflicts, the frontier becomes a stage for ghostly apparitions, time-warped duels, and the unraveling of a tapestry woven with the echoes of the past.

Just as the town begins to recover from the supernatural, a clandestine conspiracy emerges—the Eclipse Society, a shadowy organization whose influence threatens to plunge the Wild West into perpetual chaos. In a tale marked by espionage, intrigue, and covert clashes in the shadows, "Pistol Pete" must navigate a web of deceit that spans the town's influential figures, confronting both mortal adversaries and the supernatural entities unleashed by the society's dark machinations.

The pinnacle of peril awaits as the legendary figure confronts the puppetmasters behind the Eclipse Society, facing betrayal from trusted allies and initiating rituals of unbinding to counteract the society's supernatural influence. In a climactic showdown that tests the resilience of the frontier community, "Pistol Pete" emerges victorious, but the echoes of peril linger as the town rebuilds from the shadows.

Chapter 1: The Desert Dawning

In the blistering heat of the unforgiving desert, where the sun painted the vast horizon with hues of amber and gold, a lone rider kicked up the sandy trail. Dust clouds billowed behind as "Pistol Pete" Eaton guided his trusty steed, a rugged creature accustomed to the arid expanse.

Pistol Pete, a weathered figure with a face carved by years under the relentless sun, was no stranger to the harsh realities of the Wild West. His eyes, shaded by the brim of a beaten cowboy hat, scanned the barren landscape with a practiced vigilance. The wind whispered through the sparse vegetation, carrying tales of distant coyotes and the echoes of forgotten gunfights.

As Pete rode, memories of his past stirred like the desert dust. Raised on the frontier, he learned the language of the land, the subtle cues of shifting sands, and the secrets whispered by the saguaro cacti. His family, humble settlers with dreams as vast as the desert itself, instilled in him a sense of resilience.

The trail led Pistol Pete to the outskirts of a weathered town, its wooden structures weathered by time and the unforgiving elements. The saloon, with its swinging doors and weathered sign, greeted him with the promise of respite. As he dismounted, the creaking of his leather boots against the wooden boardwalk echoed through the quiet streets.

Inside the saloon, the air hung heavy with the aroma of stale whiskey and the distant hum of conversation. Pete's entrance drew fleeting glances, but the locals, engrossed in their own tales and card games, quickly returned to their business. The bartender, a stout figure with a mop of greying hair, nodded in recognition as Pete approached.

"Pistol Pete," the bartender greeted, polishing a glass with a rag that had seen better days. "Haven't seen you 'round these parts in a spell. What brings you back?"

Pete, with a half-smile playing on his weathered lips, leaned against the scarred bar. "Just the wind, Hank. It carries stories, and I reckon it's time I listened."

As Pete sipped his drink, the door swung open, revealing the silhouette of a stranger. Dust clung to the newcomer's worn boots, and the brim of a wide hat obscured their features. The tension in the saloon thickened, a silent acknowledgment of the untold stories that walked through the swinging doors.

The stranger, a figure draped in a tattered serape, sauntered toward the bar with the deliberate steps of a person carrying the weight of the frontier. The air crackled with anticipation as Pete and the newcomer exchanged nods, recognizing the shared language of those who had weathered the storms of the West.

Hank, sensing the unspoken history between the two, poured another round. "Looks like the wind brought you both here today," he remarked, his eyes flickering between Pete and the stranger.

Pete, leaning back against the bar, decided to break the silence. "What brings you to these parts?" he asked the newcomer, eyes narrowing slightly.

The stranger, with a voice as rough as the desert winds, spoke of a town besieged by outlaws, of desperate cries for justice that echoed through the canyons. Pete listened, the weight of responsibility settling on his shoulders like an old companion. The frontier, it seemed, had one more tale to tell—a tale of justice sought in the shadow of the setting sun.

As the evening sun dipped below the horizon, casting long shadows across the quiet town, Pistol Pete Eaton and the mysterious stranger left the saloon together. The trail of dust left behind bore witness to their unspoken pact, a pact to face the challenges that awaited in the untamed expanse of the Wild West. The desert night embraced them, and the stars overhead seemed to shimmer with the promise of stories yet untold.

Chapter 2: The Ambush in Shadows

After the dust settled from "Pistol Pete's" high noon showdown, the sun dipped low on the horizon, casting long shadows over the town. But in the Wild West, danger lingered like a snake in the grass.

As "Pistol Pete" sauntered down the deserted main street, the rhythmic creak of his spurs was the only sound in the still air. Little did he know, a gang of outlaws had their sights set on him.

The first warning was a flicker in the corner of his eye. Suddenly, shots rang out from the shadows—outlaws emerging like ghosts from hiding spots. "Pistol Pete" instinctively dove for cover behind a water trough as bullets whizzed past.

The town erupted into chaos once again. "Pistol Pete" returned fire, each shot a flash in the dimming light. The smell of gunpowder mixed with the metallic tang of fear as the two sides exchanged gunfire.

The outlaws, hungry for trouble, moved in with a ruthless determination. "Pistol Pete" darted from cover to cover, a master of evasion, but the outlaws were relentless. The air echoed with the thunderous roar of gunfire.

As the shadows lengthened, "Pistol Pete" realized he needed an edge. He spotted an old barrel nearby and, with a swift movement, kicked it over for makeshift cover. Bullets ricocheted off the metal, and the town seemed to shrink into a war zone.

The outlaws closed in, their shouts blending with the cacophony of gunfire. It was a high-stakes dance, each step a gamble with life and death. "Pistol Pete" knew he couldn't let these outlaws take over his town.

With a quick draw and a steady hand, "Pistol Pete" fired off a series of shots that rattled the outlaws. The tide turned as they scrambled for cover, realizing they had underestimated the legendary gunslinger.

As the last echoes of gunfire faded, "Pistol Pete" stood amidst the lingering smoke, victorious once again. The town, still and silent, bore witness to another chapter in the legend's ongoing saga.

But in the Wild West, where shadows hid secrets and danger lurked around every corner, "Pistol Pete" knew that each victory only paved the way for the next thrilling gunfight. The frontier held more challenges, and the legend of "Pistol Pete" was far from over.

Chapter 3: The Whispers of the Canyons

Days passed since Pistol Pete and the mysterious stranger rode out from the quiet town, guided by the tales carried on the desert wind. The trail led them through winding canyons, where the echoes of their horses' hooves reverberated against the towering walls of rock. The sun painted the canyon walls with warm hues, casting a mesmerizing glow on the rugged terrain.

The air hung heavy with anticipation as Pete and the stranger, their silhouettes etched against the canyon walls, pressed forward. The silence of the canyons was occasionally broken by the distant call of a hawk or the rustle of a critter navigating the rocky landscape.

Pistol Pete, his eyes scanning the horizon with a quiet determination, noticed the stranger's gaze fixed on the jagged cliffs ahead. "What's your tale, stranger?" he finally asked, breaking the quiet rhythm of hoofbeats against the dusty trail.

The stranger, still draped in the tattered serape, spoke of a past marred by shadows—of a family torn apart by the ruthless hands of outlaws. The canyon walls seemed to absorb the weight of their shared history, the wind carrying the stranger's words like leaves caught in an unseen current.

As the sun dipped lower, casting long shadows across the canyon floor, Pete and the stranger found themselves navigating a narrow pass. The walls seemed to close in, the canyon's secrets unfolding with each twist and turn. It was in these moments, amidst the solitude of the canyons, that Pete's thoughts wandered to his own past—of a homestead lost to the relentless march of time and the unyielding frontier.

The canyon path opened into a wider expanse, revealing an abandoned campsite. Charred embers lay dormant in the fire pit, a testament to those who had passed through. The stranger, their eyes scanning the surroundings, spoke of a band of outlaws that frequented the canyons, leaving a trail of chaos in their wake.

With the fading light, Pete and the stranger decided to set up camp. The horses were tethered, and a modest fire crackled to life, its warm glow flickering against the canyon walls. The stranger, their features still obscured by the wide-brimmed hat, shared tales of the outlaw gang's tactics—a cunning blend of ambushes and hit-and-run raids.

As the night deepened, the canyon seemed to come alive with unseen creatures. Pete, his gaze fixated on the dance of shadows, pondered the tangled web of fate that had brought him and the stranger together. The distant howl of a coyote echoed through the canyons, a haunting refrain that seemed to carry the stories of those who had faced the unforgiving frontier.

With the dawn breaking, Pete and the stranger packed their meager camp and resumed their journey. The canyon walls, now bathed in the soft light of morning, bore witness to the silent pact between the two. They rode deeper into the canyons, following the whispers carried on the wind—the whispers of justice sought in the heart of the untamed West.

As the sun climbed higher, casting a warm embrace over the rugged landscape, Pete and the stranger pressed forward, leaving the abandoned campsite behind. The canyons, with their towering cliffs and hidden recesses, held the promise of the next chapter in their unfolding saga—a tale yet to be written in the annals of the Wild West.

Chapter 4: Shadows on the Borderlands

The trail led Pistol Pete and the mysterious stranger through a desolate stretch of the borderlands, where the sun hung high in the cloudless sky, casting an unrelenting heat upon the arid landscape. The horizon seemed to stretch endlessly, a vast canvas of dusty trails and distant mesas.

As Pete and the stranger ventured deeper into the borderlands, the whispers of the canyons lingered in the air. The terrain became more rugged, with rocky outcrops and twisted junipers dotting the vast expanse. The horses, their hooves stirring up the fine dust, pressed forward with a steady determination.

The borderlands, a realm of extremes where life and death danced in the shimmering heat, harbored secrets known only to those who dared to tread its unforgiving paths. Pete, his eyes squinting against the harsh sunlight, sensed an invisible tension in the air. The stranger, still draped in the tattered serape, rode alongside in stoic silence.

As they approached the outskirts of a weathered town nestled on the fringes of the borderlands, Pete's gaze narrowed. The stranger, their expression unreadable beneath the wide-brimmed hat, nodded subtly. The wind carried faint echoes of life within the town—a distant hammer striking metal, the murmur of conversations, and the occasional creak of a wooden sign.

The borderlands town, a collection of adobe structures weathered by time, exuded an air of quiet resilience. Pete and the stranger guided their horses down the main street, passing by the occasional curious gaze of locals attending to their daily chores. The town's saloon, with its swinging doors and sun-bleached sign, beckoned as a hub of activity.

Inside the saloon, a motley crowd engaged in card games, conversations, and the occasional clink of glasses. The bartender, a stout figure with a mop of graying hair, looked up from cleaning a glass as Pete and the stranger entered. The atmosphere, though seemingly mundane, carried an undercurrent of tension—an unspoken understanding that the borderlands were a place where alliances were formed cautiously.

Pete approached the bar, exchanging nods with the bartender named Hank. "What brings you to these parts?" Hank inquired, his eyes flicking toward the mysterious stranger.

Pete, with a nod towards the stranger, replied, "We're here to listen, Hank. The wind carried tales, and the borderlands have a way of telling stories of their own."

The stranger, their eyes hidden beneath the shadow of the hat, spoke of the outlaws that haunted the borderlands, preying on the vulnerability of the isolated town. Pete listened intently, his thoughts drifting to the family he had lost to the merciless hands of lawless marauders—a wound that still lingered beneath the surface.

Hank, pouring a drink with a contemplative air, interjected with local rumors and sightings. The borderlands, it seemed, were a breeding ground for tales of trepidation and resilience, where the line between order and chaos blurred with each passing dust storm.

The sun dipped lower in the sky, casting long shadows across the borderlands town. Pete and the stranger, their horses tethered outside, left the saloon with a shared understanding. The borderlands, a realm of shifting sands and whispered secrets, held a chapter yet to be unveiled.

As they strolled down the quiet streets, Pete noticed the wary glances of townsfolk, their expressions a mixture of fear and curiosity. The stranger, undeterred by the scrutiny, led the way to the outskirts where the desert stretched beyond the last vestiges of civilization.

Setting up camp beneath the vast canopy of stars, Pete and the stranger shared a silent meal. The fire crackled, its warmth a comforting presence in the cool desert night. Around the flickering flames, the borderlands seemed to come alive with stories—the howls of distant coyotes, the rustle of nocturnal creatures, and the steady pulse of the wind against the sagebrush.

As the night deepened, Pete and the stranger took turns keeping watch, their eyes scanning the borderlands for any signs of approaching danger. The wind, a constant companion in the vast desert expanse, carried the night's secrets through the canyon passes and across the open plains.

Dawn painted the horizon with hues of pink and gold, heralding a new day in the borderlands. Pete and the stranger, their camp packed and horses ready, resumed their journey. The borderlands, with its silent tales and whispered warnings, awaited the justice they sought to bring—a justice written in the language of the untamed West.

Chapter 5: A Dance with the Dust Devils

The borderlands unfurled before Pistol Pete and the mysterious stranger as they ventured deeper into the sun-baked expanse. The trail ahead seemed to vanish into the shimmering waves of heat rising from the desert floor. The horses, their hooves creating a rhythmic cadence against the dusty ground, pressed forward with a determined pace.

The stranger, their silhouette framed against the vastness of the desert, led the way with a quiet assurance. The wind, a constant companion in the borderlands, carried with it the scent of sagebrush and the distant echoes of untold stories. Pete, his eyes squinting against the relentless sun, followed closely, his thoughts a mingling of anticipation and a sense of duty.

As they journeyed deeper into the borderlands, the terrain became increasingly challenging. Rocky plateaus and mesas towered on the horizon, casting elongated shadows across the rugged landscape. The stranger, draped in the tattered serape that billowed like a tamed storm, seemed attuned to the subtle shifts in the surroundings.

The trail led them to a secluded canyon, its entrance guarded by towering cliffs that seemed to touch the sky. The air within the canyon hung heavy with the promise of a story waiting to be unraveled. Pete, his senses sharpened by years in the untamed West, felt a subtle shift in the wind—an unspoken warning, perhaps, carried through the twisting passageways.

As they ventured deeper into the canyon, Pete and the stranger noticed signs of recent disturbances. Footprints in the dusty soil hinted at the passage of others—outlaws, perhaps, leaving a trail that begged to be followed. The horses, sensing the tension in the air, snorted nervously as they navigated the narrow path.

Around a bend, the canyon widened into an open expanse, revealing a makeshift camp. Tattered tents flapped in the breeze, and a solitary campfire smoldered with the remnants of a hastily abandoned meal. Pete and the stranger dismounted, their eyes scanning the surroundings for any signs of movement.

The silence of the canyon was abruptly shattered by the distant sound of approaching hooves. Dust Devils, the infamous gang rumored to haunt these borderlands, descended from the rocky ledges. Faces obscured by bandanas, they rode with a reckless abandon that sent shivers through the canyon walls.

A tension hung in the air as the Dust Devils encircled Pete and the stranger, their horses stirring up the dusty ground. The leader, distinguished by a crimson bandana and a twisted grin, signaled for a temporary ceasefire. The canyon seemed to hold its breath, awaiting the unfolding drama.

Pete, his hand instinctively resting on the hilt of his weathered six-shooter, eyed the Dust Devils with a mixture of wariness and determination. The stranger, still draped in the tattered serape that billowed like a tamed storm, stood alongside, their gaze steady.

Words were exchanged in the language of the borderlands—a mix of terse warnings and defiant challenges. The Dust Devils, driven by a lawless spirit, spoke of the untamed frontier as their domain. Pete, a guardian of justice in the wild expanse, retorted with a resolve that echoed through the canyon walls.

The ceasefire held momentarily, like a storm gathering its strength before the inevitable clash. In the uneasy calm, Pete and the stranger exchanged a glance—a silent understanding that justice in the borderlands often demanded a dance with the very shadows that sought to engulf it.

With a sudden surge, the Dust Devils launched into a reckless charge. Shots echoed through the canyon as Pete and the stranger sought cover behind the natural formations. The rocky walls became a labyrinth of refuge and peril, the canyon floor transformed into a battleground of dust and gunfire.

Pete, nimble as a desert fox, moved with a grace born of years spent navigating the intricacies of the untamed West. The stranger, their movements deliberate, fired with uncanny accuracy. The Dust Devils, fueled by their lawless intent, fired wildly, attempting to outmaneuver their formidable adversaries.

Barrels and crates, scattered across the canyon floor, offered brief respites in the relentless firefight. Shots ricocheted off the rocks as Pete and the stranger strategically repositioned themselves, anticipating the Dust Devils' moves. The once-silent canyons now reverberated with the symphony of bullets and shouts.

The leader of the Dust Devils, his crimson bandana a vivid contrast to the dusty landscape, sought out Pete in a reckless charge. The canyon seemed to hold its breath as the two gunslingers faced each other in a decisive standoff. Bullets flashed between them, the echoes of gunfire reaching a fever pitch.

In a lightning-fast draw, Pete landed a shot that sent the Dust Devils' leader sprawling. The remaining outlaws, witnessing their leader's defeat, hesitated for a fleeting moment. Seizing the opportunity, Pete and the stranger pressed the attack, chasing the retreating Dust Devils through the now-silent canyons.

As the dust settled, Pete and the stranger stood amidst the aftermath—a canyon scarred by the confrontation. The legend of the gunslinger, etched into the very rocks that bore witness, continued to echo through the borderlands. The wind, now a gentle breeze that carried the tales of the untamed West, seemed to convey a sense of justice fulfilled.

With the canyon now calm, Pete and the stranger retraced their steps, leaving the defeated Dust Devils to reckon with the consequences of their lawless pursuits. The borderlands, with its dance of shadows and stories etched into the rocky crevices, held a promise—a promise that justice, though tested by the shifting sands of time, would persist in the heart of the Wild West.

Chapter 6: Ghosts of the Ghost Town

Pistol Pete and the mysterious stranger, having quelled the storm within the borderlands, continued their journey. The sun hung low in the sky as they rode through the vast expanse, the horses' hooves creating a steady rhythm against the dusty trail. The wind, a faithful companion in the untamed West, whispered through the sagebrush, carrying tales of the journey ahead.

The trail meandered through a desolate stretch of the frontier, leading Pete and the stranger to the outskirts of a long-forgotten ghost town. Weathered buildings, their wooden structures bleached by years of exposure, stood as silent witnesses to a bygone era. The creaking of swinging doors, now rusted in place, seemed to echo through the abandoned streets.

Pete and the stranger dismounted, their boots stirring up the dust that clung to the deserted thoroughfare. The atmosphere was heavy with the weight of memories—a ghostly presence that seemed to linger among the dilapidated structures. The town, once a bustling hub of life, now stood frozen in time.

As they explored the ghost town, Pete and the stranger noticed remnants of a life interrupted. Faded signs hinted at businesses that once thrived, and shattered windows whispered tales of a past punctuated by untold struggles. The wind, carrying the melancholy of the frontier, stirred the dust in forgotten corners.

The heart of the ghost town revealed the skeletal remains of a saloon—a relic of a time when laughter and music filled its once-hallowed walls. Pete and the stranger entered cautiously, the floorboards creaking beneath their weight. The interior, bathed in a sepia-toned light filtering through the broken windows, felt like a sepulcher for memories long past.

Behind the weathered bar, bottles lined the shelves, their contents evaporated into the dry air. The silence was interrupted only by the occasional flutter of a tattered curtain or the distant call of a lone coyote. The stranger, their gaze steady, seemed to absorb the essence of the ghost town—a place where the spirits of the past coexisted with the present.

Pete, his eyes scanning the room for any signs of life, noticed a series of faded photographs on the wall. Images of families, once bound by dreams of prosperity, stared back through the sepia veil of time. Pete's thoughts drifted to his own family, the echoes of their laughter blending with the wind's mournful wail.

A sudden noise disrupted the ghostly quiet—a distant rattle, like the echoes of forgotten footsteps. Pete and the stranger exchanged glances, their instincts sharpened by the unpredictable nature of the frontier. Following the sound, they navigated the ghost town's deserted streets, the shadows of the past shifting with every step.

The noise led them to the remnants of a once-grand hotel, its faded sign bearing the name "Frontier Lodge." The door, slightly ajar, swung with a haunting creak as they entered. Inside, a flickering lantern cast long shadows on the peeling wallpaper. The air seemed charged with the presence of unseen observers.

As Pete and the stranger explored the upper floors, they stumbled upon a room that seemed frozen in time. The furniture, draped in dusty sheets, hinted at a hasty departure. A diary, its pages yellowed with age, lay open on a wooden dresser. Pete, his eyes scanning the handwritten entries, glimpsed a narrative of joy, sorrow, and the relentless march of time.

The diary told the tale of a family that once called the ghost town home—a family whose dreams were eclipsed by the shadows of the frontier. The stranger, their features still hidden beneath the wide-brimmed hat, absorbed the narrative with a quiet reverence. The ghost town, it seemed, held more than just weathered structures—it cradled the stories of lives intertwined with the unforgiving landscape.

A sudden chill filled the air as the distant rattle grew louder. Pete and the stranger, drawn by an unseen force, descended to the ghost town's outskirts. There, at the edge of the desolate streets, they discovered the source of the mysterious sound—an old piano, its keys touched by an invisible hand.

The wind, now carrying the notes of a melancholic melody, seemed to dance through the ghost town. Pete and the stranger, captivated by the spectral performance, stood in silent reverence. The piano, though weathered by time, echoed with the echoes of a bygone era—a haunting reminder of the lives that once sought solace in the heart of the frontier.

As the last notes faded into the desert breeze, the ghost town returned to its silent slumber. Pete and the stranger, moved by the ethereal experience, left the abandoned streets behind. The wind, now a gentle whisper carrying the tunes of the past, accompanied them as they rode towards the next chapter of their unfolding saga.

The sun dipped below the horizon, casting long shadows over the ghost town. The horses' hooves echoed through the empty streets as Pete and the stranger disappeared into the twilight, leaving the memories of the past to rest among the faded structures. The frontier, with its ghosts and untold tales, held more mysteries for them to unravel—a journey that stretched beyond the remnants of a forgotten town and into the heart of the boundless West.

Chapter 7: Echoes of the Mesa

Pistol Pete and the mysterious stranger rode into the vast expanse, leaving the ghost town behind. The trail led them through sprawling mesas, their towering formations reaching towards the azure sky. The sun, now descending on the horizon, cast long shadows that danced across the rugged landscape.

As they traversed the mesa's uneven terrain, Pete and the stranger felt the magnetic pull of an ancient energy—an energy that seemed to resonate with the untold tales of the land. The wind, weaving through the towering rock formations, carried with it whispers of stories etched into the stone. The horses' hooves echoed through the canyons, a symphony that harmonized with the rustling leaves and the distant calls of hidden critters.

At the base of a colossal mesa, Pete and the stranger dismounted, their eyes drawn to petroglyphs etched into the sandstone. The ancient carvings told stories of generations long past—a narrative of survival, connection, and a symbiotic dance with the untamed frontier. Pete, running his fingers over the weathered carvings, felt a connection to the spirits that lingered within the rocks.

The stranger, their gaze fixed on the mesmeric patterns, seemed to decipher the language of the petroglyphs. It was a language that spoke of challenges faced and victories won—a testament to the resilience of those who had navigated the boundless West before them. The mesa, with its silent carvings, became a portal to a time where survival meant understanding the intricate dance of nature and the relentless passage of seasons.

As the day waned, Pete and the stranger ascended the mesa, following a winding trail that snaked through the rocky outcrops. The elevation provided a panoramic view of the sprawling frontier—the undulating mesas, the patchwork of distant canyons, and the tapestry of colors painted by the setting sun. The wind, now a gentle breeze at the mesa's summit, carried with it a sense of both solitude and interconnectedness.

At the peak, Pete and the stranger found a natural alcove that offered shelter from the evening breeze. The horses, tethered nearby, grazed on the sparse vegetation that clung to the mesa's rocky surface. The stranger, their features still hidden beneath the wide-brimmed hat, seemed to commune with the ancient spirits that whispered through the canyon winds.

Around the flickering campfire, Pete and the stranger shared a simple meal—their reflections blending with the shadows cast by the dancing flames. The mesa, with its timeless energy, seemed to invite them into a communion with the land. Pete, his gaze fixed on the star-studded sky, felt a sense of humility in the face of the vast universe that stretched beyond the horizon.

As night fell over the mesa, the air filled with the haunting calls of nocturnal creatures. Pete, leaning back against the sandstone alcove, listened intently to the symphony of the night—the distant hoots of owls, the rustle of unseen critters, and the gentle hum of the wind. The stranger, still and silent, absorbed the essence of the mesa as if communing with the very spirits that had left their mark on the stone canvas.

In the quiet of the mesa's summit, Pete and the stranger took turns keeping watch over the slumbering frontier. The stars overhead seemed to blink in approval, their light filtering through the ancient petroglyphs. The mesa, with its timeless tales etched into the rock, stood as a sentinel overlooking the vast expanse.

As the night deepened, Pete and the stranger found solace in the shared silence. The wind, a gentle caress against the mesa's sandstone face, carried with it the promise of a new day. With the first light of dawn, they descended from the summit, leaving the ancient carvings to be kissed by the morning sun.

As they resumed their journey across the mesas, Pete and the stranger felt a newfound connection to the untamed West—a connection forged by the echoes of the mesa and the spirits that lingered within its rocky embrace. The wind, now a steadfast companion, carried with it the stories of the land—a land that held mysteries, challenges, and the boundless beauty of the Wild West.

The mesas, with their towering presence and silent carvings, became waypoints in the unfolding saga of Pistol Pete and the mysterious stranger. As they rode into the horizon, the wind continued to carry the echoes of the mesa—whispers of resilience, whispers of timelessness, and the eternal tales etched into the very heart of the frontier.

Chapter 8: The Crossing at Coyote Creek

Pistol Pete and the mysterious stranger, their journey through the mesas behind them, rode towards the distant horizon. The trail led them through a vast expanse dotted with sagebrush, the horses' hooves creating a rhythmic symphony against the dusty ground. The sun, a golden orb in the cloudless sky, cast a warm glow over the sprawling frontier.

As they rode, Pete and the stranger approached the banks of Coyote Creek—a winding watercourse that carved through the landscape. The sound of flowing water and the rustling leaves of cottonwood trees signaled the presence of life amidst the vastness of the frontier. The creek, its banks lined with vibrant wildflowers, seemed to beckon the weary travelers to its refreshing embrace.

Pete and the stranger, guided by the winding trail, reached the edge of Coyote Creek. The horses, sensing the proximity of water, neighed with anticipation. Pete, his eyes scanning the surroundings, noticed a weathered wooden bridge spanning the creek—a crossing worn by countless travelers before them. The stranger, draped in the tattered serape, led the way towards the bridge.

Upon reaching the creek's edge, Pete and the stranger dismounted. The horses, grateful for the respite, drank from the crystal-clear waters. The stranger, their gaze fixed on the meandering course of the creek, seemed to absorb the tranquility of the scene. The air was filled with the melody of nature—the babbling of the creek, the chirping of crickets, and the distant call of a mockingbird.

As they approached the bridge, Pete noticed weathered planks and faded paint—a testament to the countless journeys that had crossed this threshold. The bridge, though showing signs of age, stood sturdy and reliable, a silent witness to the ebb and flow of the untamed West. Pete and the stranger exchanged a glance, a silent acknowledgment of the crossing that lay ahead.

Midway across the bridge, Pete and the stranger paused. The creek flowed beneath them, its waters reflecting the azure sky. Pete, his gaze fixated on the rippling current, felt a sense of introspection—a realization that each crossing held its own significance in the vast tapestry of the frontier.

As they continued their journey, Pete and the stranger reached the other side of Coyote Creek. The landscape unfolded before them, a patchwork of rolling hills and distant canyons. The wind, carrying the scent of sagebrush and the promise of new horizons, seemed to urge them forward. The horses, refreshed from their drink, eagerly pressed on.

The trail, now leading through a series of hills, offered panoramic views of the expansive frontier. Pete and the stranger rode side by side, the mesas and canyons blending into a mosaic of earthy hues. The stranger, their eyes hidden beneath the wide-brimmed hat, spoke in sparse words of the journey and the mysteries that lay ahead.

As they ascended a hill, the landscape shifted once again. A valley unfolded before them, carpeted with golden grasses that swayed in the breeze. A herd of antelope grazed in the distance, their graceful movements adding to the serenity of the scene. Pete and the stranger, now immersed in the tranquility of the valley, allowed themselves a moment of respite.

Setting up a modest camp in the valley, Pete and the stranger gathered around a crackling fire. The warmth of the flames, a companion in the cool evening, cast flickering shadows on the valley floor. The stranger, their features illuminated by the dancing light, shared tales of the frontier—of uncharted territories, hidden oases, and the unyielding spirit of those who called the Wild West home.

As night descended over the valley, the stars painted the sky with their brilliant glow. Pete and the stranger, their silhouettes outlined against the celestial canvas, contemplated the vastness of the frontier. The valley, cradled between the hills, seemed to hold its breath as if participating in the silent conversation between the two travelers.

Under the blanket of stars, Pete and the stranger took turns keeping watch over the valley. The wind, a gentle lullaby in the quiet night, carried with it the promise of new beginnings. The frontier, with its ever-changing landscapes and unspoken tales, held a chapter yet to be written.

With the first light of dawn, Pete and the stranger broke camp and resumed their journey. The valley, now bathed in the soft hues of morning, bid farewell to the travelers as they ventured towards the next horizon. Coyote Creek, with its crossing and the serenity of the valley, became waypoints in the unfolding saga—a saga written in the language of the untamed West, where each trail, each crossing, carried the echoes of the frontier's eternal song.

Chapter 9: Shadows of the Whispering Pines

Pistol Pete and the mysterious stranger, their horses forging a path through the undulating terrain, continued their journey into the heart of the frontier. The trail led them into a dense forest of whispering pines, the towering trees casting dappled shadows on the forest floor. The air, fragrant with the scent of pine needles, held an enchanting stillness that seemed to echo with the secrets of the woods.

As they ventured deeper into the forest, the sunlight filtered through the thick canopy, creating a mosaic of light and shade. The horses, their hooves muffled by the pine needles carpeting the ground, moved with a quiet grace. Pete and the stranger, their eyes alert to the nuances of the wooded expanse, navigated the labyrinth of towering trunks and winding trails.

The stranger, draped in the tattered serape, seemed attuned to the whispers of the pines—an unseen guide through the shadows that danced beneath the branches. Pete, his senses sharpened by years in the wild, noticed the subtle shifts in the forest—a rustle in the underbrush, the distant call of a bird, and the occasional scampering of woodland creatures.

As they followed the trail, Pete and the stranger reached a clearing bathed in the soft glow of filtered sunlight. The clearing, surrounded by ancient pines, seemed to hold a timeless quality—a sanctuary within the heart of the forest. The horses, sensing the tranquility of the space, grazed contentedly on the lush grass.

In the center of the clearing stood an ancient stone well, its moss-covered surface attesting to its age. Pete, drawn to the well by an unseen force, approached and peered into its depths. The water, clear as crystal, reflected the surrounding pines and seemed to hold the secrets of the forest within its liquid embrace.

The stranger, standing alongside Pete, gestured towards the well with a subtle nod. It was as if the well, with its mysterious allure, beckoned them to listen to the whispers of the pines and the tales woven into the fabric of the forest. Pete, his hand trailing through the cool water, felt a connection to the untamed beauty that surrounded them.

As the day progressed, Pete and the stranger decided to rest in the clearing—a respite beneath the ancient pines. The horses, tethered nearby, found shade beneath the towering trees. The stranger, their features partially revealed by the dappled sunlight, shared tales of the forest—of creatures that roamed in the moonlit hours, of hidden springs that quenched the thirst of both man and beast, and of the mystical energy that permeated the wooded expanse.

In the quiet of the forest, a soft breeze stirred the pine needles overhead. The trees, their branches forming a natural canopy, whispered tales of the ancient spirits that guarded the heart of the wilderness. Pete, leaning against the rough bark of a pine, absorbed the essence of the forest—a place where time seemed to stand still, and the rustling leaves spoke in a language known only to those who listened with their hearts.

As evening descended, Pete and the stranger kindled a campfire in the clearing. The flames, dancing in the gathering dusk, cast a warm glow that pushed back the encroaching shadows. The stranger, their gaze fixed on the flickering embers, shared stories of the hidden trails that crisscrossed the forest—a network of winding paths that connected distant corners of the untamed frontier.

Under the starlit sky, Pete and the stranger marveled at the celestial display overhead. The whispering pines, their branches forming a cathedral-like ceiling, seemed to invite the travelers into a silent communion with the cosmos. The night, punctuated by the soft calls of nocturnal creatures, unfolded in a timeless dance between shadow and light.

As they slept beneath the whispering pines, Pete and the stranger dreamt of the forest's secrets—the ancient tales etched into the bark, the spirits that danced among the branches, and the ever-changing symphony of the wild. The forest, with its enigmatic allure, cradled them in its embrace, weaving their dreams into the very fabric of the untamed West.

With the first light of dawn, Pete and the stranger bid farewell to the clearing and the whispering pines. The trail, now leading them out of the forest, promised new landscapes and the mysteries yet to be unveiled. The horses, their coats dappled with the morning dew, eagerly pressed on, carrying the echoes of the forest within the hoofbeats that resonated through the boundless frontier. The shadows of the whispering pines, though left behind, lingered in the hearts of the travelers as they rode towards the next chapter of their unfolding saga.

Chapter 10: Serenade of the Silver Canyon

Pistol Pete and the mysterious stranger rode out of the whispering pines, the forest's enigmatic embrace lingering in the air as they ventured deeper into the frontier. The trail led them towards the horizon, where the landscape transitioned into a vast stretch of canyons and mesas. The sun, a radiant orb in the expansive sky, cast a warm glow over the ever-changing tableau of the Wild West.

As they rode, the terrain shifted beneath the hooves of their horses. The trail guided them towards the entrance of Silver Canyon—a majestic ravine whose walls gleamed with the silver hues of the exposed rock. The air, now filled with the scent of sagebrush and the promise of adventure, hummed with an energy unique to the canyons that crisscrossed the untamed frontier.

Pete and the stranger approached the canyon's edge, where the trail descended into its depths. The horses, sure-footed companions in the rugged landscape, carefully navigated the winding path. As they descended, the walls of Silver Canyon rose like ancient sentinels, their silver veins shimmering in the sunlight.

Midway through the descent, the canyon widened into a breathtaking vista. The trail led them to a natural amphitheater—a vast expanse surrounded by towering rock formations. The stranger, draped in the tattered serape, seemed to sense the significance of the canyon's embrace. Pete, his eyes scanning the panoramic view, felt a sense of reverence for the majesty that unfolded before them.

In the heart of Silver Canyon, the travelers decided to make camp. The horses, tethered on a flat plateau, gazed out over the expansive canyon floor. The stranger, their features partially revealed by the wide-brimmed hat, gestured towards the surrounding rock formations—a silent invitation to explore the secrets hidden within the silver-hued walls.

As the sun dipped below the canyon rim, Pete and the stranger explored the labyrinthine passages of Silver Canyon. The walls, sculpted by centuries of wind and water, seemed to tell a tale of resilience and transformation. Petroglyphs, etched into the rock by hands long gone, hinted at the lives that had once sought shelter within the canyon's embrace.

In a secluded alcove, Pete and the stranger discovered a natural spring—a crystalline pool fed by underground veins. The water, cool and refreshing, mirrored the silver hues of the canyon walls. The stranger, their eyes reflecting the colors of the rock, approached the spring with a quiet reverence. Pete, his hands cupped to drink, felt a connection to the lifeblood that flowed within the heart of Silver Canyon.

As night fell, the canyon transformed into a celestial canvas. The stars, brilliant in the absence of city lights, painted the sky with their twinkling glow. Pete and the stranger, seated on a ledge overlooking the canyon floor, marveled at the cosmic display. The wind, carrying with it the echoes of the untamed West, whispered through the rock formations as if adding its voice to the serenade of the night.

Around the campfire, the stranger shared tales of Silver Canyon—of ancient tribes that sought refuge within its walls, of the elusive wildlife that roamed its floor, and of the enduring spirit that echoed through the silver veins of the rock. Pete, his gaze fixed on the dancing flames, absorbed the stories that wove the canyon into the very fabric of the frontier.

As the fire burned low, Pete and the stranger settled into a comfortable silence. The canyon, bathed in moonlight, held a timeless allure—a place where the boundaries between earth and sky seemed to blur. The night, punctuated by the distant calls of nocturnal creatures, wrapped the travelers in its gentle embrace.

With the first light of dawn, Pete and the stranger bid farewell to Silver Canyon. The trail, now leading them out of the rock labyrinth, promised new landscapes and challenges. The horses, rested and ready, carried the echoes of the canyon within their hoofbeats as they ventured towards the next chapter of their unfolding saga.

Silver Canyon, with its silver-hued walls and ancient tales, became a waypoint in the journey of Pistol Pete and the mysterious stranger. The wind, now a steadfast companion, carried with it the serenade of the canyon—a melodic reminder of the untamed beauty that awaited them beyond the rocky embrace. As they rode towards the horizon, the whispers of Silver Canyon echoed in their hearts, blending with the symphony of the Wild West that stretched before them.

Chapter 11: Whispers in the Whirlwind

Pistol Pete and the mysterious stranger rode out of the embrace of Silver Canyon, the echoes of the silver-hued walls fading behind them as they ventured into the expanse of the untamed frontier. The trail wound through rolling hills and expansive meadows, the horses' hooves creating a rhythmic melody against the canvas of the open landscape. The sun, a golden disc in the vast sky, bathed the frontier in a warm glow.

As they rode, the terrain gradually transformed into a sweeping plain dotted with tufts of grass and patches of wildflowers. The wind, a constant companion in the Wild West, began to pick up, carrying with it the whispers of distant tales. Pete and the stranger, their eyes scanning the horizon, felt the change in the air—a prelude to the mysteries that awaited them in the heart of the frontier.

The trail led them towards a distant mesa, its silhouette rising against the expansive sky like a sentinel guarding the secrets of the land. As they approached, the wind intensified, swirling dust devils danced across the plain, creating an otherworldly spectacle. The stranger, their serape billowing in the gusts, seemed to commune with the elements—a silent acknowledgment of the untamed forces that shaped the frontier.

At the base of the mesa, the horses slowed as the trail began to ascend. Pete and the stranger climbed higher, the panoramic view unfolding before them. The mesa, a plateau of red rock, offered a commanding vantage point over the sprawling frontier. The wind, now a constant companion, carried the scent of the earth and the distant promise of adventure.

On the mesa's summit, Pete and the stranger dismounted. The land stretched in all directions—a vast tapestry of hills, canyons, and distant mesas. The stranger, their gaze fixed on the horizon, seemed to sense the presence of something beyond the visible—a force that resonated with the very essence of the untamed West. Pete, leaning against a weathered boulder, took in the expansive view, feeling the power of the land beneath his fingertips.

As the day unfolded, Pete and the stranger explored the mesa's surface. Ancient petroglyphs adorned the red rock, telling stories of the land's vibrant past. The stranger, tracing the lines with a weathered hand, seemed to decipher the language of the symbols—a narrative of the cycles of nature, the dance of celestial bodies, and the enduring spirit of those who had walked the frontier before.

In a secluded alcove, they discovered a collection of weathered bones—a relic of a time when the mesa served as a hunting ground for ancient tribes. Pete, his fingers brushing the sun-bleached remains, felt a connection to the primal forces that had shaped the land. The wind, carrying with it the whispers of bygone eras, seemed to murmur tales of survival, challenges, and the ever-changing dance of life.

As the sun dipped below the horizon, casting long shadows over the mesa, Pete and the stranger made camp. The horses grazed on the sparse vegetation, and a campfire crackled in the cool evening air. The stranger, their face partially obscured by the flickering flames, shared stories of the mesa—of forgotten rituals, celestial observations, and the symbiotic relationship between the land and its inhabitants.

Under the canopy of stars, Pete and the stranger lay on the mesa's surface, their gazes fixed on the cosmic display overhead. The wind, now a gentle breeze, carried with it the haunting calls of nocturnal creatures. The mesa, with its ancient tales and whispered secrets, became a sanctuary for contemplation—a place where the boundaries between earth and sky blurred.

As they slept beneath the celestial dome, Pete and the stranger dreamt of the whispers in the whirlwind—the unseen forces that shaped the frontier and guided their journey. The night, with its symphony of celestial bodies and ethereal calls, cradled them in its embrace.

With the first light of dawn, Pete and the stranger bid farewell to the mesa. The trail, now leading them down from the plateau, promised new landscapes and challenges. The horses, their coats gleaming in the morning sun, carried the echoes of the mesa within their hoofbeats as they ventured towards the next chapter of their unfolding saga.

The mesa, with its timeless stories etched in rock and bone, became a waypoint in the journey of Pistol Pete and the mysterious stranger. The wind, a steadfast companion, carried with it the whispers of the whirlwind—a melodic reminder of the invisible forces that shaped the Wild West. As they rode towards the next horizon, the echoes of the mesa lingered in their hearts, blending with the ongoing symphony of the untamed West that stretched before them.

Chapter 12: Dance of the Desert Spirits

Pistol Pete and the mysterious stranger rode on from the mesa, their horses weaving through the changing landscape of the untamed frontier. The trail led them into the vastness of the desert—a sea of golden sand dunes stretching as far as the eye could see. The sun, a blazing orb in the cloudless sky, painted the desert with hues of amber and gold.

As they journeyed through the shifting sands, the horses' hooves left imprints on the desert floor. The air, dry and filled with the scent of sun-baked earth, seemed to vibrate with the energy of the desert. Pete and the stranger, their faces shielded from the sun by wide-brimmed hats, pressed on into the heart of the arid expanse.

In the distance, mirages shimmered on the horizon—a play of light and heat that teased the senses. The stranger, seemingly attuned to the secrets of the desert, guided the way through the undulating dunes. Pete, squinting against the sunlight, marveled at the beauty of the seemingly endless sea of sand.

As they rode deeper into the desert, Pete and the stranger noticed a distant formation of rocks rising from the sands. The wind, now carrying with it the soft whispers of the desert spirits, seemed to guide them towards the rocky outcrop. The horses, their ears perked in anticipation, quickened their pace as if drawn by an unseen force.

Upon reaching the rocks, Pete and the stranger discovered a hidden oasis—a small pool of clear water surrounded by hardy desert vegetation. The horses, grateful for the respite, drank from the oasis. Pete and the stranger, removing their hats to feel the cool breeze, took in the oasis's unexpected beauty in the midst of the relentless desert.

In the shade of the rocks, they decided to rest. The stranger, their gaze fixed on the shimmering heat waves in the distance, seemed lost in contemplation. Pete, wiping the sweat from his brow, felt the calming energy of the oasis—a sanctuary in the midst of the harsh desert. The wind, a gentle caress against the rocks, carried with it the tales of survival and resilience written in the very sands beneath their feet.

As the day wore on, Pete and the stranger explored the rocky formation. Petroglyphs adorned the weathered surfaces—symbols and shapes etched by the hands of those who had sought refuge in the desert's embrace. The stranger, their fingers tracing the ancient carvings, seemed to decipher the language of the rocks—a narrative of endurance, adaptation, and the unbroken spirit of the desert dwellers.

In the late afternoon, the duo climbed to the top of the rocks, where a panoramic view of the desert unfolded before them. The dunes, now bathed in the warm hues of the setting sun, stretched like waves frozen in time. The stranger, standing on the rocky precipice, raised their arms as if communing with the desert spirits that danced in the fading light.

As evening descended over the desert, Pete and the stranger made camp near the oasis. The horses, now rested and content, grazed on the resilient desert plants. The stranger, draped in the tattered serape, shared stories of the desert—of nomadic tribes that navigated the shifting sands, of hidden oases that sustained life in the arid expanse, and of the timeless dance between earth and sky.

Under the canopy of stars, Pete and the stranger sat around the campfire. The desert, now bathed in the soft glow of moonlight, seemed to come alive with unseen spirits. The stranger, their voice a rhythmic cadence in the quiet night, spoke of the desert's mysteries—the mirages that deceived, the spirits that whispered in the wind, and the enduring beauty that thrived in the most unexpected corners of the arid wilderness.

As they slept beneath the starlit sky, Pete and the stranger dreamt of the dance of the desert spirits—the ethereal figures that wove tales in the sands and spoke in the language of the wind. The night, with its celestial spectacle and the haunting calls of nocturnal creatures, cradled them in its embrace.

With the first light of dawn, Pete and the stranger bid farewell to the oasis and the rocks that stood as sentinels in the desert. The trail, now leading them away from the dunes, promised new landscapes and challenges. The horses, their coats dusted with the sands of the desert, carried the echoes of the oasis within their hoofbeats as they ventured towards the next chapter of their unfolding saga.

The desert, with its silent whispers and hidden oases, became a waypoint in the journey of Pistol Pete and the mysterious stranger. The wind, now a constant companion, carried with it the tales of the desert spirits—a melodic reminder of the unseen forces that shaped the Wild West. As they rode towards the next horizon, the echoes of the desert lingered in their hearts, blending with the ongoing symphony of the untamed frontier that stretched before them.

Chapter 13: Veil of the Ghostly Canyons

Pistol Pete and the mysterious stranger rode onward, leaving the desert oasis behind as the trail wound through the ever-changing landscape of the untamed frontier. The terrain shifted once again, leading them towards the jagged outlines of distant canyons. The sun, now casting long shadows in the late afternoon, painted the rocky walls with hues of orange and red.

As they approached the canyons, Pete and the stranger noticed a peculiar quality to the landscape. The air seemed to shimmer with an ethereal light, and the distant canyons appeared almost as if veiled in a translucent curtain. The stranger, their gaze fixed on the ghostly canyons, seemed to sense the enigmatic nature of the terrain. Pete, squinting against the sun's glare, felt a sense of anticipation as they ventured deeper into the canyonlands.

The trail led them into a labyrinth of narrow passages and towering cliffs. The horses, their hooves echoing in the rocky corridors, navigated the maze with a sure-footed grace. Pete and the stranger, their eyes scanning the walls for signs of ancient stories, entered a canyon that seemed to resonate with an otherworldly energy.

As they rode deeper into the canyon, the air grew cooler, and the light took on a surreal quality. Shadows played on the rock surfaces, creating illusions that danced in the corners of Pete's vision. The stranger, riding ahead, seemed to become one with the shifting shadows, their silhouette blending with the spectral hues of the canyon.

Midway through the canyon, they discovered a natural amphitheater—a circular space surrounded by towering cliffs. In the center, a pool of water reflected the ghostly light. Pete and the stranger, drawn to the eerie beauty of the place, dismounted and approached the pool. The water, clear as crystal, seemed to hold a mirror to the mysteries concealed within the canyon's depths.

As they lingered in the amphitheater, a soft breeze whispered through the canyon, carrying with it the echoes of ghostly tales. Pete and the stranger, seated on a flat rock, felt the energy of the place—a convergence of the tangible and the intangible. The stranger, draped in the tattered serape, gestured towards the cliffs, inviting Pete to listen to the stories written in the layers of rock.

In the shifting light of dusk, Pete and the stranger made camp in the amphitheater. The horses, tethered near the pool, grazed on the sparse vegetation that clung to the canyon walls. The stranger, their eyes fixed on the star-studded sky, began to share tales of the ghostly canyons—of ancient spirits that inhabited the rocky passages, of echoes that transcended time, and of the unspoken language spoken by the wind through the canyon corridors.

Under the celestial dome, Pete and the stranger lay on their bed-rolls, gazing at the stars that shimmered above the ghostly canyons. The night, silent save for the occasional rustle of the breeze, held a mystical quality. The stranger, their voice carrying the weight of ancient tales, spoke of the unseen forces that governed the canyonlands—the spirits that danced in the shadows, the phantoms that carved tales in the rock, and the timeless energy that pulsed through the very heart of the ghostly canyons.

As they slept beneath the starlit sky, Pete and the stranger dreamt of the veiled mysteries of the canyon—a realm where the boundaries between the living and the spectral blurred. The night, with its ethereal presence and the haunting calls of distant creatures, cradled them in its embrace.

With the first light of dawn, Pete and the stranger bid farewell to the ghostly canyons. The trail, now leading them out of the labyrinthine passages, promised new landscapes and challenges. The horses, their coats shimmering with the remnants of the spectral light, carried the echoes of the canyon within their hoofbeats as they ventured towards the next chapter of their unfolding saga.

The ghostly canyons, with their veiled beauty and ethereal tales, became a waypoint in the journey of Pistol Pete and the mysterious stranger. The wind, now a whispering guide, carried with it the echoes of the spectral realm—a melodic reminder of the unseen forces that shaped the Wild West. As they rode towards the next horizon, the mysteries of the ghostly canyons lingered in their hearts, blending with the ongoing symphony of the untamed frontier that stretched before them.

Chapter 14: Echoes of the Forgotten Citadel

Pistol Pete and the mysterious stranger, their journey weaving through the diverse tapestry of the untamed frontier, continued towards the next enigmatic destination. The trail led them away from the ghostly canyons, guiding them into a vast expanse of plains and hills. The sun, now hanging low in the western sky, cast a warm glow over the ever-changing landscape.

As they rode, the terrain gradually transformed into a series of low hills crowned with clusters of ancient trees. The stranger, their gaze scanning the horizon, seemed to sense a presence in the air—a subtle vibration that hinted at the proximity of something significant. Pete, his eyes attuned to the details of the frontier, followed the stranger's lead as they approached a distant rise.

At the crest of the hill, a sight unfolded before them—a forgotten citadel, its weathered walls rising against the backdrop of the setting sun. The stranger, their silhouette framed by the golden light, gestured towards the ancient structure. Pete, his curiosity piqued, urged his horse forward as they descended towards the forgotten citadel.

The citadel, surrounded by a ring of weathered stones, stood as a silent testament to a bygone era. Vines climbed the crumbling walls, and the echoes of a distant past seemed to linger in the air. Pete and the stranger, their horses treading softly over the overgrown path, approached the entrance of the citadel.

As they entered, the interior revealed a maze of corridors and chambers, each bearing the scars of time. Faded murals adorned the walls, telling tales of battles, celebrations, and the daily life of those who once inhabited the citadel. Pete, running his fingers over the ancient artwork, felt a connection to the lives that had unfolded within the forgotten walls.

In the central courtyard, a dilapidated fountain stood—a relic of a time when water flowed freely within the citadel. The stranger, their eyes reflecting the melancholy of the ruins, approached the fountain with a sense of reverence. Pete, surveying the crumbling architecture, imagined the vibrant scenes that once played out in the shadow of the citadel's towering walls.

The citadel, with its mysterious aura, seemed to invite exploration. Pete and the stranger ascended a weathered staircase that led to the highest tower. From the summit, the view stretched across the expansive frontier—the hills, the plains, and the distant canyons painted in the warm hues of the setting sun. The stranger, their gaze fixed on the horizon, seemed to commune with the echoes of a forgotten era.

As the daylight waned, Pete and the stranger decided to make camp within the citadel. The horses, tethered in the courtyard, grazed on the wild grass that pushed through the ancient stones. The stranger, draped in the tattered serape, kindled a campfire that flickered in the gathering darkness. Pete, his eyes scanning the starlit sky, felt the weight of the citadel's history—the untold stories and the enduring spirit of the forgotten realm.

Around the campfire, the stranger shared tales of the citadel—of a civilization that once thrived in harmony with the land, of the struggles that led to its eventual decline, and of the mysteries that still lingered within the crumbling walls. Pete, his gaze fixed on the dancing flames, absorbed the stories that wove the citadel into the very fabric of the untamed frontier.

Under the celestial dome, Pete and the stranger lay on their bedrolls within the citadel's courtyard. The night, silent save for the occasional rustle of leaves and the distant calls of nocturnal creatures, held a contemplative stillness. The citadel, with its ancient tales and forgotten whispers, became a sanctuary for reflection—a place where time seemed to stand still.

As they slept beneath the starlit sky, Pete and the stranger dreamt of the echoes of the forgotten citadel—the voices of those who had once walked its halls, the celebrations that had echoed through its chambers, and the resilience that had marked its slow descent into the annals of history. The night, with its ethereal presence and the haunting calls of the nocturnal creatures, cradled them in its embrace.

With the first light of dawn, Pete and the stranger bid farewell to the forgotten citadel. The trail, now leading them away from the ruins, promised new landscapes and challenges. The horses, their coats brushed by the morning dew, carried the echoes of the citadel within their hoofbeats as they ventured towards the next chapter of their unfolding saga.

The forgotten citadel, with its tales etched in stone and memory, became a waypoint in the journey of Pistol Pete and the mysterious stranger. The wind, now a gentle breeze, carried with it the echoes of the ancient realm—a melodic reminder of the enduring spirit that lingered within the forgotten walls. As they rode towards the next horizon, the mysteries of the citadel lingered in their hearts, blending with the on-going symphony of the untamed frontier that stretched before them.

Chapter 15: The Enchanted Grove

Pistol Pete and the mysterious stranger, their journey through the untamed frontier a continuous tapestry of discovery, left the forgotten citadel behind and followed the trail as it meandered through rolling hills and dense woods. The landscape transitioned into a lush expanse, filled with the vibrant colors of wildflowers and the sweet scent of blossoming trees. The sun, filtering through the thick canopy of leaves, created dappled patterns on the forest floor.

As they rode, the horses' hooves kicked up earthy fragrances, and the air became tinged with the refreshing aroma of the woods. Pete and the stranger, their senses attuned to the natural symphony around them, entered a realm untouched by time—a place that seemed to vibrate with an enchanting energy.

The trail led them deeper into the heart of the forest, where ancient trees towered overhead, their branches interwoven to create a natural cathedral of greenery. Birds, their melodies blending with the rustle of leaves, flitted from branch to branch. The stranger, their eyes reflecting the play of sunlight and shadows, seemed to recognize the enchantment woven into the grove.

Amidst the towering trees, Pete and the stranger stumbled upon a hidden glade—an open space surrounded by ancient oaks and adorned with a carpet of moss. In the center, a crystal-clear stream murmured its way through smooth stones. The horses, sensing the magic of the place, approached the stream to drink. Pete and the stranger dismounted, drawn to the serenity that enveloped the enchanted grove.

The stranger, their hand outstretched, brushed against the leaves of an ancient oak, as if greeting an old friend. Pete, his senses heightened by the mystical aura, felt a connection to the natural energy that pulsed through the grove. The air seemed to hum with life, and the vibrant colors of the wildflowers held an intensity that bordered on the otherworldly.

As they explored the grove, Pete and the stranger discovered a circle of standing stones near the stream—a hidden sanctuary within the heart of the enchanted woods. The stranger, their fingers tracing the weathered surfaces, seemed to commune with the ancient spirits that lingered in the moss-covered stones. Pete, captivated by the silent conversation, felt the presence of something beyond the tangible—the whispers of nature's guardians.

In the midst of the grove, they decided to make camp. The horses grazed on the lush grass, and a small fire crackled, casting a warm glow over the enchanting surroundings. The stranger, draped in the tattered serape, began to share tales of the enchanted grove—of a time when ancient civilizations revered the spirits of the woods, of the magic that coursed through the very veins of the land, and of the enduring bond between humanity and nature.

Under the verdant canopy, Pete and the stranger sat around the campfire. The grove, now bathed in the soft glow of moonlight filtering through the leaves, seemed to come alive with unseen spirits. The stranger, their voice a melodic cadence in the quiet night, spoke of the interconnected web of life—the dance of fireflies, the rustle of nocturnal creatures, and the ethereal beauty that thrived in the heart of the enchanted woods.

As they slept beneath the celestial canopy, Pete and the stranger dreamt of the enchantment that pulsed through the grove—the ancient spirits that whispered in the wind, the dance of moonlight on the moss-covered stones, and the timeless connection between humanity and the natural world. The night, with its magical presence and the soothing calls of nocturnal creatures, cradled them in its embrace.

With the first light of dawn, Pete and the stranger bid farewell to the enchanted grove. The trail, now leading them out of the mystical woods, promised new landscapes and challenges. The horses, their coats brushed by the morning dew, carried the echoes of the grove within their hoofbeats as they ventured towards the next chapter of their unfolding saga.

The enchanted grove, with its timeless magic and natural wonders, became a waypoint in the journey of Pistol Pete and the mysterious stranger. The wind, now a gentle whisper, carried with it the melodies of the woods—a melodic reminder of the interconnected dance of life that unfolded in the heart of the untamed frontier. As they rode towards the next horizon, the enchantment of the grove lingered in their hearts, blending with the ongoing symphony of the untamed wilderness that stretched before them.

Chapter 16: Whispers of the Twilight Mesa

Pistol Pete and the mysterious stranger, their journey carrying them through a myriad of landscapes, followed the trail as it led them towards a distant mesa bathed in the soft hues of twilight. The sun, now a crimson orb on the horizon, cast long shadows across the expansive plains. The air, cooler as the day surrendered to evening, carried with it the subtle transition between day and night.

As they approached the twilight mesa, the terrain shifted to a series of low hills, and the horses navigated their way through the undulating landscape. The stranger, their gaze fixed on the distant silhouette of the mesa, seemed to sense a unique energy emanating from the twilight-draped heights. Pete, his senses attuned to the subtle shifts in the frontier, shared a knowing glance with the stranger as they rode on.

The trail led them to the base of the mesa, where the soft glow of twilight painted the rock formations with shades of lavender and indigo. The horses, their hooves creating a rhythmic cadence against the rocky ground, carried Pete and the stranger towards the ascent. The mesa, a sentinel in the fading light, seemed to beckon them to explore its secrets.

As they climbed higher, the panorama unfolded before them. The twilight mesa offered a breathtaking view of the surrounding landscape—the rolling hills, the distant canyons, and the plains stretching towards the horizon. Pete and the stranger, their gazes captivated by the twilight-drenched tableau, felt a sense of awe at the beauty that unfolded beneath the canvas of the evening sky.

On the mesa's summit, a gentle breeze greeted them. The air, tinged with the scent of juniper and sage, seemed to carry the whispers of the twilight—a time when the boundary between day and night blurred. The stranger, their face touched by the last rays of sunlight, stood as if in communion with the evolving hues of the frontier. Pete, leaning against a weathered boulder, took in the expansive view, feeling the serenity of the mesa seep into his very being.

As the day transitioned to night, Pete and the stranger made camp on the mesa's summit. The horses, tethered nearby, grazed on the sparse vegetation that clung to the rocky surface. The stranger, their gaze fixed on the emerging stars, began to share tales of the twilight mesa—of a place where ancient tribes gathered to observe celestial events, of the spirits that roamed the mesa during the transition between light and darkness, and of the enduring connection between the land and its inhabitants.

Under the celestial dome, Pete and the stranger sat around the campfire. The mesa, now bathed in the silvery light of the moon, seemed to hold a quiet reverence for the unfolding night. The stranger, their voice a soothing cadence in the quietude, spoke of the tales etched in the mesa's stones—the cycles of celestial bodies, the ancient rituals that marked the passage of time, and the symbiotic relationship between the land and those who called it home.

As they slept beneath the starlit sky, Pete and the stranger dreamt of the whispers of the twilight mesa—the unseen forces that guided the frontier through the veil of night, the dance of shadows on the mesa's surface, and the timeless energy that pulsed through the very heart of the twilight-draped heights. The night, with its celestial ballet and the haunting calls of nocturnal creatures, cradled them in its embrace.

With the first light of dawn, Pete and the stranger bid farewell to the twilight mesa. The trail, now leading them down from the summit, promised new landscapes and challenges. The horses, their coats gleaming in the morning light, carried the echoes of the mesa within their hoofbeats as they ventured towards the next chapter of their unfolding saga.

The twilight mesa, with its serene beauty and celestial tales, became a waypoint in the journey of Pistol Pete and the mysterious stranger. The wind, now a gentle whisper, carried with it the melodies of the twilight—a melodic reminder of the seamless dance between day and night that unfolded in the untamed frontier. As they rode towards the next horizon, the whispers of the twilight mesa lingered in their hearts, blending with the ongoing symphony of the ever-changing wilderness that stretched before them.

Chapter 17: Dance of the Prairie Spirits

Pistol Pete and the mysterious stranger, their trail winding through the vast frontier, continued their journey as the landscape transitioned into expansive prairies stretching towards the distant horizon. The sun, now a golden disc in the high noon sky, painted the undulating grasslands with hues of amber and gold. The air, filled with the sweet scent of wildflowers and the distant calls of prairie birds, carried the energy of the untamed wilderness.

As they rode, the horses' hooves created a rhythmic beat against the soft earth, and the prairie winds whispered secrets that danced through the tall grass. The stranger, their eyes scanning the vastness of the plains, seemed attuned to the spirits that roamed the prairie—a realm where the untamed and the ethereal coexisted. Pete, his senses immersed in the openness of the landscape, shared a silent understanding with the stranger as they traversed the endless sea of grass.

The trail led them to a place where the prairie seemed to undulate in a natural rhythm—a vast expanse where the grasses swayed in unison with the wind. In the center, a circle of ancient stones marked a sacred space on the prairie canvas. The horses, sensing the sanctity of the place, approached the stone circle with a quiet reverence. Pete and the stranger dismounted, drawn to the energy that pulsed within the prairie dance floor.

In the midst of the stone circle, Pete and the stranger felt the heartbeat of the prairie—the pulse of the land that had witnessed countless seasons and the cyclical dance of life. The stranger, their movements mirroring the sway of the grasses, seemed to become one with the prairie spirits. Pete, his boots sinking into the soft earth, embraced the primal connection to the untamed wilderness.

As they stood in the sacred circle, the wind carried with it the haunting calls of distant creatures—the unseen inhabitants of the prairie. The stranger, their hands outstretched, gestured towards the horizon, inviting Pete to witness the dance of the prairie spirits. The grasses, now caught in an invisible choreography, moved with a grace that seemed to transcend the physical realm.

In the heart of the prairie dance floor, Pete and the stranger decided to make camp. The horses, content in the sacred space, grazed on the lush grasses. The stranger, draped in the tattered serape, kindled a campfire that crackled in the evening air. Pete, sitting on a weathered stone, felt the presence of the prairie spirits—a force that wove through the very fabric of the untamed landscape.

Around the campfire, the stranger shared tales of the prairie spirits —of ancient legends that spoke of the guardians of the grasslands, of the ethereal dances that unfolded under the vast sky, and of the timeless energy that connected the inhabitants of the prairie to the land itself. Pete, his gaze fixed on the flames, absorbed the stories that painted a vivid picture of the untamed spirits that breathed life into the prairie.

Under the starlit sky, Pete and the stranger lay on their bedrolls within the stone circle. The night, with its celestial spectacle and the haunting calls of nocturnal creatures, held a sense of communion with the prairie spirits. The stranger, their voice a melodic whisper in the quietude, spoke of the unseen forces that guided the prairie dance—the spirits that reveled in the moonlight, the echoes that resonated through the grasses, and the enduring connection between humanity and the untamed wilderness.

As they slept beneath the celestial dome, Pete and the stranger dreamt of the dance of the prairie spirits—the ethereal figures that wove tales in the grass, the rhythms that pulsed through the very heart of the plains, and the timeless energy that connected all living things on the prairie. The night, with its ethereal presence and the soothing calls of distant creatures, cradled them in its embrace.

With the first light of dawn, Pete and the stranger bid farewell to the prairie dance floor. The trail, now leading them away from the stone circle, promised new landscapes and challenges. The horses, their coats brushed by the morning dew, carried the echoes of the prairie spirits within their hoofbeats as they ventured towards the next chapter of their unfolding saga.

The prairie dance floor, with its timeless rhythms and untamed spirits, became a waypoint in the journey of Pistol Pete and the mysterious stranger. The wind, now a gentle breeze, carried with it the melodies of the prairie—a melodic reminder of the harmonious dance that unfolded under the expansive sky. As they rode towards the next horizon, the echoes of the prairie spirits lingered in their hearts, blending with the ongoing symphony of the ever-changing wilderness that stretched before them.

Chapter 18: Shadows of the Mesquite Grove

Pistol Pete and the mysterious stranger, their journey through the vast frontier an ever-unfolding saga, found themselves guided by the trail into a mesquite grove as the sun dipped below the western horizon. The air, warm with the remnants of the day, carried the sweet fragrance of mesquite blossoms. The horses, their hooves stirring the soft earth, navigated the shadowy pathways of the grove with an innate familiarity.

The stranger, their eyes attuned to the shifting patterns of light and shade, led Pete into the heart of the mesquite grove. The tall, gnarled trees cast elongated shadows on the ground, creating a dance of darkness and moonlit patches. Pete, his senses alive to the subtle nuances of the frontier, felt a mystical aura enveloping the grove—an energy that seemed to linger within the interwoven branches.

As they ventured deeper, the mesquite grove revealed hidden clearings adorned with silvery moonlight. The stranger, their silhouette blending with the shadows, moved with an ethereal grace as they explored the labyrinthine pathways. Pete, his boots crunching softly on the dry earth, marveled at the enchanting beauty that unfolded beneath the mesquite canopy.

In the heart of the grove, they discovered a natural amphitheater—a circular space surrounded by ancient mesquite trees. The stranger, their hand tracing the rough bark of one of the trees, seemed to commune with the spirits that resided within the grove. Pete, his eyes scanning the shadowy alcoves, felt a sense of reverence for the untamed energy that pulsed through the mesquite grove.

The horses, sensing the sacredness of the place, grazed on the sparse grasses within the amphitheater. Pete and the stranger, seated on a fallen log, observed the dance of shadows and moonlight that played out on the mesquite branches. The stranger, draped in the tattered serape, began to share tales of the mesquite grove—of a place where spirits found solace in the cool shadows, where echoes whispered through the rustling leaves, and where the moonlit nights held a special kind of magic.

Under the celestial canopy, Pete and the stranger decided to make camp within the mesquite grove. The horses, tethered near the clearing, became companions in the quietude of the night. The stranger, their voice carrying the weight of ancient tales, spoke of the mesquite spirits—of the guardians that watched over the grove, of the ethereal dance that unfolded under the moonlit sky, and of the timeless connection between the land and those who traversed its shadows.

Around the campfire, the mesquite grove seemed to come alive with unseen energies. The stranger's stories painted vivid pictures of the spirits that called the grove home—the whispers that carried messages on the night breeze, the shadows that danced in the moonlight, and the ancient tales etched in the very roots of the mesquite trees. Pete, his gaze fixed on the flickering flames, absorbed the stories that resonated with the mystical heart of the grove.

As they slept beneath the starlit sky, Pete and the stranger dreamt of the shadows of the mesquite grove—the spirits that moved through the moonlit branches, the ancient rhythms that echoed within the clearing, and the timeless energy that connected all living things in the heart of the frontier. The night, with its ethereal presence and the haunting calls of distant creatures, cradled them in its embrace.

With the first light of dawn, Pete and the stranger bid farewell to the mesquite grove. The trail, now leading them out of the labyrinthine pathways, promised new landscapes and challenges. The horses, their coats brushed by the morning dew, carried the echoes of the mesquite spirits within their hoofbeats as they ventured towards the next chapter of their unfolding saga.

The mesquite grove, with its shadowy beauty and ancient spirits, became a waypoint in the journey of Pistol Pete and the mysterious stranger. The wind, now a gentle whisper, carried with it the melodies of the grove—a melodic reminder of the timeless dance between light and shadow that unfolded in the untamed frontier. As they rode towards the next horizon, the shadows of the mesquite grove lingered in their hearts, blending with the ongoing symphony of the ever-changing wilderness that stretched before them.

Chapter 19: Veins of the Silver Canyon

Pistol Pete and the mysterious stranger, their trail leading them through the intricate tapestry of the frontier, embarked on a new leg of their journey that wound into the heart of the Silver Canyon. The sun, now climbing the eastern sky, cast its warm rays over the rugged terrain. The air, tinged with the scent of sagebrush and anticipation, carried with it the promise of untold tales hidden within the canyon's walls.

As they approached the entrance of the Silver Canyon, the trail transformed into a narrow passageway flanked by towering cliffs. The horses, sure-footed in the rocky terrain, navigated the winding path with a steady determination. The stranger, their gaze scanning the intricate patterns in the canyon walls, seemed to sense the ancient secrets etched into the very stones of the canyon. Pete, his eyes tracing the contours of the rugged landscape, shared a silent acknowledgment with the stranger as they ventured deeper into the Silver Canyon.

The canyon walls, made of silver-hued stone, seemed to gleam with a natural brilliance as they rose majestically on either side. The path beneath their hooves, worn smooth by centuries of travelers, led Pete and the stranger further into the depths of the canyon. The trail, carved by the persistent force of water over eons, spoke of the timeless journey that had shaped the very essence of the Silver Canyon.

As they progressed, the canyon widened, revealing a network of side passages and hidden alcoves. Pete and the stranger, guided by an un-spoken understanding, explored the intricate veins of the Silver Canyon —the twists and turns that beckoned them to uncover the mysteries concealed within the heart of the rugged landscape.

In one of the canyon's alcoves, they discovered a natural spring—a crystalline pool fed by underground veins of water. The horses, their coats reflecting the silver hues of the canyon walls, drank from the re-freshing pool. Pete and the stranger, their thirst quenched by the pure water, felt a connection to the lifeblood that flowed through the very veins of the Silver Canyon.

Further along the trail, the canyon walls seemed to close in, creating a narrow passage known as the Silver Gorge. The horses, their hooves echoing against the canyon walls, carried Pete and the stranger through the shadowy embrace of the gorge. The stranger, their eyes scanning the rugged terrain, guided the way with a quiet confidence. Pete, leaning into the curves of the canyon, marveled at the natural architecture that surrounded them.

As they emerged from the Silver Gorge, the canyon widened once again, revealing a sprawling basin bathed in sunlight. The Silver Can-yon, with its veins of silver-hued stone and hidden alcoves, held a sense of reverence for the forces that had sculpted its timeless beauty. Pete and the stranger, their senses heightened by the grandeur of the canyon, felt a connection to the enduring spirit that flowed through the very veins of the untamed wilderness.

In the heart of the Silver Canyon, Pete and the stranger decided to make camp. The horses, tethered in a sheltered alcove, grazed on the sparse vegetation that clung to the canyon floor. The stranger, draped in the tattered serape, kindled a campfire that flickered in the evening light. Pete, sitting on a flat rock, absorbed the tranquil ambiance of the canyon—the whispers of the wind, the rustle of leaves, and the distant calls of canyon-dwelling creatures.

Around the campfire, the stranger shared tales of the Silver Canyon —of the veins of silver that had drawn prospectors in search of fortune, of the ancient ceremonies held within its hidden alcoves, and of the enduring spirit that flowed through the very heart of the rugged landscape. Pete, his gaze fixed on the dancing flames, absorbed the stories that painted a vivid picture of the untamed forces that had shaped the Silver Canyon through the ages.

As they slept beneath the starlit sky, Pete and the stranger dreamt of the veins of the Silver Canyon—the ancient currents that pulsed through the very stones, the echoes of footsteps that had traversed the winding paths, and the timeless energy that connected all living things in the heart of the rugged landscape. The night, with its celestial brilliance and the haunting calls of nocturnal creatures, cradled them in its embrace.

With the first light of dawn, Pete and the stranger bid farewell to the Silver Canyon. The trail, now leading them out of the basin, promised new landscapes and challenges. The horses, their coats shimmering in the morning sun, carried the echoes of the canyon within their hoofbeats as they ventured towards the next chapter of their unfolding saga.

The Silver Canyon, with its veins of silver-hued stone and hidden alcoves, became a waypoint in the journey of Pistol Pete and the mysterious stranger. The wind, now a gentle breeze, carried with it the melodies of the canyon—a melodic reminder of the enduring spirit that flowed through the very veins of the untamed frontier. As they rode towards the next horizon, the veins of the Silver Canyon lingered in their hearts, blending with the ongoing symphony of the ever-changing wilderness that stretched before them.

Chapter 20: Whispers of the Mystic Oasis

Pistol Pete and the mysterious stranger, their journey through the untamed frontier a kaleidoscope of landscapes, found themselves drawn towards the Mystic Oasis—a legendary sanctuary nestled amidst the sprawling wilderness. The sun, now ascending the azure sky, cast its golden rays over the landscape. The air, tinged with the fragrance of wildflowers and the anticipation of discovery, carried with it the promise of the mystical haven that awaited them.

As they approached the entrance to the Mystic Oasis, the trail led them through a series of lush meadows adorned with vibrant blooms. The horses, their hooves creating a soft melody against the earth, carried Pete and the stranger into a realm where the boundaries between reality and enchantment seemed to blur. The stranger, their eyes reflecting the awe-inspiring beauty around them, led Pete towards the heart of the oasis with a quiet assurance.

The meadows gave way to a dense thicket, and as they passed through, the air became cooler, filled with the refreshing scent of a hidden spring. Emerging from the thicket, Pete and the stranger beheld the Mystic Oasis—an emerald jewel cradled within the embrace of ancient trees. A natural pool, fed by crystal-clear waters, sparkled in the dappled sunlight. Exotic flowers adorned the edges, their colors reflecting the vibrancy of the untamed wilderness.

The stranger, their gaze fixed on the oasis, seemed to commune with the unseen forces that guarded the sacred waters. Pete, his senses attuned to the mystical aura, felt a profound connection to the oasis—a haven where the magic of the frontier revealed itself in all its splendor.

As they approached the pool, the horses, sensing the sanctity of the oasis, drank from the clear waters. Pete and the stranger, drawn to the tranquility of the place, dipped their hands into the pool, feeling the cool embrace of the mystic waters. The oasis, with its timeless beauty, held an air of serenity that seemed to transcend the hurried pace of the outside world.

In the heart of the Mystic Oasis, they discovered a natural stone platform surrounded by weeping willows. The stranger, their fingers tracing the patterns on the ancient stones, invited Pete to join them in a moment of reflection. The horses, now resting in the shade, added to the harmonious atmosphere with their occasional neighs and contented grazing.

The stranger, draped in the tattered serape, began to share tales of the Mystic Oasis—of a place where weary travelers found respite, of the spirits that guarded the sacred waters, and of the mystical rituals held under the canopy of ancient trees. Pete, his eyes fixed on the tranquil pool, absorbed the stories that painted a vivid picture of the timeless magic that pervaded the oasis.

As the day unfolded into evening, Pete and the stranger decided to make camp within the Mystic Oasis. The horses, content in the peaceful surroundings, found their own spots to rest. The stranger, kindling a campfire with wood gathered from the outskirts of the oasis, cast a warm glow over the scene. Pete, sitting on a moss-covered rock, felt the mystic energies of the oasis enveloping him—a comforting embrace that seemed to harmonize with the very essence of the untamed frontier.

Around the campfire, the stranger shared tales of the mystical rituals held within the Mystic Oasis—the dances that honored the spirits, the whispers that carried messages on the evening breeze, and the timeless connection between those who sought solace and the enchanted waters. Pete, his gaze fixed on the flickering flames, absorbed the stories that resonated with the ancient rhythms of the oasis.

As they slept beneath the celestial dome, Pete and the stranger dreamt of the whispers of the Mystic Oasis—the unseen forces that moved through the rustling leaves, the reflections that danced on the surface of the pool, and the timeless energy that connected all living things in the heart of the enchanted sanctuary. The night, with its celestial brilliance and the soothing calls of nocturnal creatures, cradled them in its embrace.

With the first light of dawn, Pete and the stranger bid farewell to the Mystic Oasis. The trail, now leading them away from the sacred waters, promised new landscapes and challenges. The horses, their coats glistening in the morning light, carried the echoes of the oasis within their hoofbeats as they ventured towards the next chapter of their unfolding saga.

The Mystic Oasis, with its emerald waters and ancient stones, became a waypoint in the journey of Pistol Pete and the mysterious stranger. The wind, now a gentle breeze, carried with it the melodies of the oasis—a melodic reminder of the timeless magic that flowed through the very heart of the untamed frontier. As they rode towards the next horizon, the whispers of the Mystic Oasis lingered in their hearts, blending with the ongoing symphony of the ever-changing wilderness that stretched before them.

The Legend Of Pistol Pete
By
Doug Hensley
Table Of Contents

Chapter 1: The Trail Begins

- Introduction to Pistol Pete and the mysterious stranger
- Pete's life as a scout and his encounter with the stranger
- Mysterious events hinting at the untamed frontier

Chapter 2: Shadows of the Mesquite Grove

- Pete and the stranger explore the mystical mesquite grove
- Encounter with ancient spirits and tales of the grove
- Unveiling the stranger's enigmatic past

Chapter 3: Veins of the Silver Canyon

- Journey into the heart of the Silver Canyon
- Discovery of silver-hued stone and hidden alcoves
- Encounters with frontier challenges and adversaries

Chapter 4: Whispers of the Mystic Oasis

- Arrival at the legendary Mystic Oasis

- Exploration of the enchanted waters and surrounding meadows
- Uncovering the oasis's mystical history

Chapter 5: Dance of the Prairie Spirits

- Riding through vast prairies and discovering sacred stone circles
- Connection to the prairie spirits and their untold stories
- Pete's growing awareness of his role in the frontier's tapestry

Chapter 6: Secrets of the Whispering Pines

- Trekking through dense pine forests
- Encounters with mysterious figures and creatures
- Whispering pines revealing ancient secrets

Chapter 7: Echoes in the Caverns of Time

- Delving into mysterious caverns
- Discovery of ancient cave paintings and artifacts
- Time-traveling elements revealing the untamed past

Chapter 8: Storm on the Horizon

- Dark clouds gather as a storm approaches
- Challenges intensify, testing Pete and the stranger
- Unraveling of personal histories amid adversity

Chapter 9: The Sentinel Peaks

- Ascending towering peaks to gain a vantage point
- Observing the vastness of the frontier
- Revelations about the journey and its purpose

Chapter 10: Enchantment of the Moonlit Marsh

- Navigating through a surreal marsh under the moonlight
- Encounter with mystical creatures and guardian spirits
- Pete and the stranger confronting inner fears

Chapter 11: Fireside Tales and Revelations

- Campfire discussions revealing deeper truths
- Sharing personal stories and motives
- Strengthening the bond between Pete and the stranger

Chapter 12: Spirits of the Forgotten Ghost Town

- Stumbling upon a ghost town with a haunted history
- Interactions with lingering spirits
- Confrontations with the unresolved past

Chapter 13: Shadows Across the Sand Dunes

- Crossing expansive sand dunes under the scorching sun
- Mirage-like encounters and illusions
- Pete's resilience and determination tested

Chapter 14: Celestial Harmony in the Starlit Sky

- Nights spent under the vast celestial dome
- Reflections on the interconnectedness of the universe
- Pete and the stranger seeking guidance from the stars

Chapter 15: Serenade of the Waterfall

- Discovering a majestic waterfall hidden within the wilderness

- Renewal and cleansing amid the cascading waters
- The waterfall as a symbol of hope and rebirth

Chapter 16: Labyrinth of the Enchanted Lagoon

- Navigating through a labyrinthine lagoon surrounded by bio-luminescent flora
- Encounter with mystical creatures and ancient guardians
- The lagoon as a passage to the next phase of the journey

17: Guardians of the Forgotten Temple

- Stumbling upon a forgotten temple in the heart of the frontier
- Confronting guardians and deciphering ancient rites
- Pete and the stranger's roles in the temple's mystery

Chapter 18: The Eldritch Winds

- Journey through a desolate landscape marked by eerie winds
- Encounter with eldritch forces and ethereal entities
- Unraveling the connection between Pete and the stranger

Chapter 19: Echoes of the Final Confrontation

- Gathering storm as Pete and the stranger face ultimate challenges
- Showdown with adversaries from the past
- Revelations leading to the climax of the journey

Chapter 20: The Unending Frontier

- Resolution and aftermath of the journey
- Pete and the stranger part ways, each carrying the lessons of the frontier

- Closing the chapter on the untamed wilderness, leaving it forever imprinted on their souls.

Author's Notes

In the heart of the untamed Wild West, where the dust of the frontier conceals secrets as ancient as the land itself, emerges a legendary figure known only as "Pistol Pete." In "Pistol Pete's Odyssey," embark on a gripping journey that transcends the boundaries of folklore, weaving together supernatural encounters, temporal anomalies, and clandestine conspiracies that shape the destiny of a frontier town.

As mysterious forces stir beneath the starlit skies, "Pistol Pete" becomes the town's vigilant guardian, confronting a host of enigmatic adversaries that defy mortal comprehension. From a bone-chilling encounter with the ancient Wendigo to navigating the delicate balance between celestial anomalies and temporal rifts, the legendary figure faces challenges that test not only his marksmanship but the very fabric of reality.

The narrative unfolds with a spectral lament that echoes through the Wild West, leading "Pistol Pete" on a journey through forgotten legacies and ethereal realms. As the haunting strains reveal untold stories and unresolved conflicts, the frontier becomes a stage for ghostly apparitions, time-warped duels, and the unraveling of a tapestry woven with the echoes of the past.

Just as the town begins to recover from the supernatural, a clandestine conspiracy emerges—the Eclipse Society, a shadowy organization whose influence threatens to plunge the Wild West into perpetual chaos. In a tale marked by espionage, intrigue, and covert clashes in the shadows, "Pistol Pete" must navigate a web of deceit that spans the town's influential figures, confronting both mortal adversaries and the supernatural entities unleashed by the society's dark machinations.

The pinnacle of peril awaits as the legendary figure confronts the puppetmasters behind the Eclipse Society, facing betrayal from trusted allies and initiating rituals of unbinding to counteract the society's supernatural influence. In a climactic showdown that tests the resilience of the frontier community, "Pistol Pete" emerges victorious, but the echoes of peril linger as the town rebuilds from the shadows.

Chapter 1: The Desert Dawning

In the blistering heat of the unforgiving desert, where the sun painted the vast horizon with hues of amber and gold, a lone rider kicked up the sandy trail. Dust clouds billowed behind as "Pistol Pete" Eaton guided his trusty steed, a rugged creature accustomed to the arid expanse.

Pistol Pete, a weathered figure with a face carved by years under the relentless sun, was no stranger to the harsh realities of the Wild West. His eyes, shaded by the brim of a beaten cowboy hat, scanned the barren landscape with a practiced vigilance. The wind whispered through the sparse vegetation, carrying tales of distant coyotes and the echoes of forgotten gunfights.

As Pete rode, memories of his past stirred like the desert dust. Raised on the frontier, he learned the language of the land, the subtle cues of shifting sands, and the secrets whispered by the saguaro cacti. His family, humble settlers with dreams as vast as the desert itself, instilled in him a sense of resilience.

The trail led Pistol Pete to the outskirts of a weathered town, its wooden structures weathered by time and the unforgiving elements. The saloon, with its swinging doors and weathered sign, greeted him with the promise of respite. As he dismounted, the creaking of his leather boots against the wooden boardwalk echoed through the quiet streets.

Inside the saloon, the air hung heavy with the aroma of stale whiskey and the distant hum of conversation. Pete's entrance drew fleeting glances, but the locals, engrossed in their own tales and card games, quickly returned to their business. The bartender, a stout figure with a mop of greying hair, nodded in recognition as Pete approached.

"Pistol Pete," the bartender greeted, polishing a glass with a rag that had seen better days. "Haven't seen you 'round these parts in a spell. What brings you back?"

Pete, with a half-smile playing on his weathered lips, leaned against the scarred bar. "Just the wind, Hank. It carries stories, and I reckon it's time I listened."

As Pete sipped his drink, the door swung open, revealing the silhouette of a stranger. Dust clung to the newcomer's worn boots, and the brim of a wide hat obscured their features. The tension in the saloon thickened, a silent acknowledgment of the untold stories that walked through the swinging doors.

The stranger, a figure draped in a tattered serape, sauntered toward the bar with the deliberate steps of a person carrying the weight of the frontier. The air crackled with anticipation as Pete and the newcomer exchanged nods, recognizing the shared language of those who had weathered the storms of the West.

Hank, sensing the unspoken history between the two, poured another round. "Looks like the wind brought you both here today," he remarked, his eyes flickering between Pete and the stranger.

Pete, leaning back against the bar, decided to break the silence. "What brings you to these parts?" he asked the newcomer, eyes narrowing slightly.

The stranger, with a voice as rough as the desert winds, spoke of a town besieged by outlaws, of desperate cries for justice that echoed through the canyons. Pete listened, the weight of responsibility settling on his shoulders like an old companion. The frontier, it seemed, had one more tale to tell—a tale of justice sought in the shadow of the setting sun.

As the evening sun dipped below the horizon, casting long shadows across the quiet town, Pistol Pete Eaton and the mysterious stranger left the saloon together. The trail of dust left behind bore witness to their unspoken pact, a pact to face the challenges that awaited in the untamed expanse of the Wild West. The desert night embraced them, and the stars overhead seemed to shimmer with the promise of stories yet untold.

Chapter 2: The Ambush in Shadows

After the dust settled from "Pistol Pete's" high noon showdown, the sun dipped low on the horizon, casting long shadows over the town. But in the Wild West, danger lingered like a snake in the grass.

As "Pistol Pete" sauntered down the deserted main street, the rhythmic creak of his spurs was the only sound in the still air. Little did he know, a gang of outlaws had their sights set on him.

The first warning was a flicker in the corner of his eye. Suddenly, shots rang out from the shadows—outlaws emerging like ghosts from hiding spots. "Pistol Pete" instinctively dove for cover behind a water trough as bullets whizzed past.

The town erupted into chaos once again. "Pistol Pete" returned fire, each shot a flash in the dimming light. The smell of gunpowder mixed with the metallic tang of fear as the two sides exchanged gunfire.

The outlaws, hungry for trouble, moved in with a ruthless determination. "Pistol Pete" darted from cover to cover, a master of evasion, but the outlaws were relentless. The air echoed with the thunderous roar of gunfire.

As the shadows lengthened, "Pistol Pete" realized he needed an edge. He spotted an old barrel nearby and, with a swift movement, kicked it over for makeshift cover. Bullets ricocheted off the metal, and the town seemed to shrink into a war zone.

The outlaws closed in, their shouts blending with the cacophony of gunfire. It was a high-stakes dance, each step a gamble with life and death. "Pistol Pete" knew he couldn't let these outlaws take over his town.

With a quick draw and a steady hand, "Pistol Pete" fired off a series of shots that rattled the outlaws. The tide turned as they scrambled for cover, realizing they had underestimated the legendary gunslinger.

As the last echoes of gunfire faded, "Pistol Pete" stood amidst the lingering smoke, victorious once again. The town, still and silent, bore witness to another chapter in the legend's ongoing saga.

But in the Wild West, where shadows hid secrets and danger lurked around every corner, "Pistol Pete" knew that each victory only paved the way for the next thrilling gunfight. The frontier held more challenges, and the legend of "Pistol Pete" was far from over.

Chapter 3: The Whispers of the Canyons

Days passed since Pistol Pete and the mysterious stranger rode out from the quiet town, guided by the tales carried on the desert wind. The trail led them through winding canyons, where the echoes of their horses' hooves reverberated against the towering walls of rock. The sun painted the canyon walls with warm hues, casting a mesmerizing glow on the rugged terrain.

The air hung heavy with anticipation as Pete and the stranger, their silhouettes etched against the canyon walls, pressed forward. The silence of the canyons was occasionally broken by the distant call of a hawk or the rustle of a critter navigating the rocky landscape.

Pistol Pete, his eyes scanning the horizon with a quiet determination, noticed the stranger's gaze fixed on the jagged cliffs ahead. "What's your tale, stranger?" he finally asked, breaking the quiet rhythm of hoofbeats against the dusty trail.

The stranger, still draped in the tattered serape, spoke of a past marred by shadows—of a family torn apart by the ruthless hands of outlaws. The canyon walls seemed to absorb the weight of their shared history, the wind carrying the stranger's words like leaves caught in an unseen current.

As the sun dipped lower, casting long shadows across the canyon floor, Pete and the stranger found themselves navigating a narrow pass. The walls seemed to close in, the canyon's secrets unfolding with each twist and turn. It was in these moments, amidst the solitude of the canyons, that Pete's thoughts wandered to his own past—of a homestead lost to the relentless march of time and the unyielding frontier.

The canyon path opened into a wider expanse, revealing an abandoned campsite. Charred embers lay dormant in the fire pit, a testament to those who had passed through. The stranger, their eyes scanning the surroundings, spoke of a band of outlaws that frequented the canyons, leaving a trail of chaos in their wake.

With the fading light, Pete and the stranger decided to set up camp. The horses were tethered, and a modest fire crackled to life, its warm glow flickering against the canyon walls. The stranger, their features still obscured by the wide-brimmed hat, shared tales of the outlaw gang's tactics—a cunning blend of ambushes and hit-and-run raids.

As the night deepened, the canyon seemed to come alive with unseen creatures. Pete, his gaze fixated on the dance of shadows, pondered the tangled web of fate that had brought him and the stranger together. The distant howl of a coyote echoed through the canyons, a haunting refrain that seemed to carry the stories of those who had faced the unforgiving frontier.

With the dawn breaking, Pete and the stranger packed their meager camp and resumed their journey. The canyon walls, now bathed in the soft light of morning, bore witness to the silent pact between the two. They rode deeper into the canyons, following the whispers carried on the wind—the whispers of justice sought in the heart of the untamed West.

As the sun climbed higher, casting a warm embrace over the rugged landscape, Pete and the stranger pressed forward, leaving the abandoned campsite behind. The canyons, with their towering cliffs and hidden recesses, held the promise of the next chapter in their unfolding saga—a tale yet to be written in the annals of the Wild West.

Chapter 4: Shadows on the Borderlands

The trail led Pistol Pete and the mysterious stranger through a desolate stretch of the borderlands, where the sun hung high in the cloudless sky, casting an unrelenting heat upon the arid landscape. The horizon seemed to stretch endlessly, a vast canvas of dusty trails and distant mesas.

As Pete and the stranger ventured deeper into the borderlands, the whispers of the canyons lingered in the air. The terrain became more rugged, with rocky outcrops and twisted junipers dotting the vast expanse. The horses, their hooves stirring up the fine dust, pressed forward with a steady determination.

The borderlands, a realm of extremes where life and death danced in the shimmering heat, harbored secrets known only to those who dared to tread its unforgiving paths. Pete, his eyes squinting against the harsh sunlight, sensed an invisible tension in the air. The stranger, still draped in the tattered serape, rode alongside in stoic silence.

As they approached the outskirts of a weathered town nestled on the fringes of the borderlands, Pete's gaze narrowed. The stranger, their expression unreadable beneath the wide-brimmed hat, nodded subtly. The wind carried faint echoes of life within the town—a distant hammer striking metal, the murmur of conversations, and the occasional creak of a wooden sign.

The borderlands town, a collection of adobe structures weathered by time, exuded an air of quiet resilience. Pete and the stranger guided their horses down the main street, passing by the occasional curious gaze of locals attending to their daily chores. The town's saloon, with its swinging doors and sun-bleached sign, beckoned as a hub of activity.

Inside the saloon, a motley crowd engaged in card games, conversations, and the occasional clink of glasses. The bartender, a stout figure with a mop of graying hair, looked up from cleaning a glass as Pete and the stranger entered. The atmosphere, though seemingly mundane, carried an undercurrent of tension—an unspoken understanding that the borderlands were a place where alliances were formed cautiously.

Pete approached the bar, exchanging nods with the bartender named Hank. "What brings you to these parts?" Hank inquired, his eyes flicking toward the mysterious stranger.

Pete, with a nod towards the stranger, replied, "We're here to listen, Hank. The wind carried tales, and the borderlands have a way of telling stories of their own."

The stranger, their eyes hidden beneath the shadow of the hat, spoke of the outlaws that haunted the borderlands, preying on the vulnerability of the isolated town. Pete listened intently, his thoughts drifting to the family he had lost to the merciless hands of lawless marauders—a wound that still lingered beneath the surface.

Hank, pouring a drink with a contemplative air, interjected with local rumors and sightings. The borderlands, it seemed, were a breeding ground for tales of trepidation and resilience, where the line between order and chaos blurred with each passing dust storm.

The sun dipped lower in the sky, casting long shadows across the borderlands town. Pete and the stranger, their horses tethered outside, left the saloon with a shared understanding. The borderlands, a realm of shifting sands and whispered secrets, held a chapter yet to be unveiled.

As they strolled down the quiet streets, Pete noticed the wary glances of townsfolk, their expressions a mixture of fear and curiosity. The stranger, undeterred by the scrutiny, led the way to the outskirts where the desert stretched beyond the last vestiges of civilization.

Setting up camp beneath the vast canopy of stars, Pete and the stranger shared a silent meal. The fire crackled, its warmth a comforting presence in the cool desert night. Around the flickering flames, the borderlands seemed to come alive with stories—the howls of distant coyotes, the rustle of nocturnal creatures, and the steady pulse of the wind against the sagebrush.

As the night deepened, Pete and the stranger took turns keeping watch, their eyes scanning the borderlands for any signs of approaching danger. The wind, a constant companion in the vast desert expanse, carried the night's secrets through the canyon passes and across the open plains.

Dawn painted the horizon with hues of pink and gold, heralding a new day in the borderlands. Pete and the stranger, their camp packed and horses ready, resumed their journey. The borderlands, with its silent tales and whispered warnings, awaited the justice they sought to bring—a justice written in the language of the untamed West.

Chapter 5: A Dance with the Dust Devils

The borderlands unfurled before Pistol Pete and the mysterious stranger as they ventured deeper into the sun-baked expanse. The trail ahead seemed to vanish into the shimmering waves of heat rising from the desert floor. The horses, their hooves creating a rhythmic cadence against the dusty ground, pressed forward with a determined pace.

The stranger, their silhouette framed against the vastness of the desert, led the way with a quiet assurance. The wind, a constant companion in the borderlands, carried with it the scent of sagebrush and the distant echoes of untold stories. Pete, his eyes squinting against the relentless sun, followed closely, his thoughts a mingling of anticipation and a sense of duty.

As they journeyed deeper into the borderlands, the terrain became increasingly challenging. Rocky plateaus and mesas towered on the horizon, casting elongated shadows across the rugged landscape. The stranger, draped in the tattered serape that billowed like a tamed storm, seemed attuned to the subtle shifts in the surroundings.

The trail led them to a secluded canyon, its entrance guarded by towering cliffs that seemed to touch the sky. The air within the canyon hung heavy with the promise of a story waiting to be unraveled. Pete, his senses sharpened by years in the untamed West, felt a subtle shift in the wind—an unspoken warning, perhaps, carried through the twisting passageways.

As they ventured deeper into the canyon, Pete and the stranger noticed signs of recent disturbances. Footprints in the dusty soil hinted at the passage of others—outlaws, perhaps, leaving a trail that begged to be followed. The horses, sensing the tension in the air, snorted nervously as they navigated the narrow path.

Around a bend, the canyon widened into an open expanse, revealing a makeshift camp. Tattered tents flapped in the breeze, and a solitary campfire smoldered with the remnants of a hastily abandoned meal. Pete and the stranger dismounted, their eyes scanning the surroundings for any signs of movement.

The silence of the canyon was abruptly shattered by the distant sound of approaching hooves. Dust Devils, the infamous gang rumored to haunt these borderlands, descended from the rocky ledges. Faces obscured by bandanas, they rode with a reckless abandon that sent shivers through the canyon walls.

A tension hung in the air as the Dust Devils encircled Pete and the stranger, their horses stirring up the dusty ground. The leader, distinguished by a crimson bandana and a twisted grin, signaled for a temporary ceasefire. The canyon seemed to hold its breath, awaiting the unfolding drama.

Pete, his hand instinctively resting on the hilt of his weathered six-shooter, eyed the Dust Devils with a mixture of wariness and determination. The stranger, still draped in the tattered serape that billowed like a tamed storm, stood alongside, their gaze steady.

Words were exchanged in the language of the borderlands—a mix of terse warnings and defiant challenges. The Dust Devils, driven by a lawless spirit, spoke of the untamed frontier as their domain. Pete, a guardian of justice in the wild expanse, retorted with a resolve that echoed through the canyon walls.

The ceasefire held momentarily, like a storm gathering its strength before the inevitable clash. In the uneasy calm, Pete and the stranger exchanged a glance—a silent understanding that justice in the borderlands often demanded a dance with the very shadows that sought to engulf it.

With a sudden surge, the Dust Devils launched into a reckless charge. Shots echoed through the canyon as Pete and the stranger sought cover behind the natural formations. The rocky walls became a labyrinth of refuge and peril, the canyon floor transformed into a battleground of dust and gunfire.

Pete, nimble as a desert fox, moved with a grace born of years spent navigating the intricacies of the untamed West. The stranger, their movements deliberate, fired with uncanny accuracy. The Dust Devils, fueled by their lawless intent, fired wildly, attempting to outmaneuver their formidable adversaries.

Barrels and crates, scattered across the canyon floor, offered brief respites in the relentless firefight. Shots ricocheted off the rocks as Pete and the stranger strategically repositioned themselves, anticipating the Dust Devils' moves. The once-silent canyons now reverberated with the symphony of bullets and shouts.

The leader of the Dust Devils, his crimson bandana a vivid contrast to the dusty landscape, sought out Pete in a reckless charge. The canyon seemed to hold its breath as the two gunslingers faced each other in a decisive standoff. Bullets flashed between them, the echoes of gunfire reaching a fever pitch.

In a lightning-fast draw, Pete landed a shot that sent the Dust Devils' leader sprawling. The remaining outlaws, witnessing their leader's defeat, hesitated for a fleeting moment. Seizing the opportunity, Pete and the stranger pressed the attack, chasing the retreating Dust Devils through the now-silent canyons.

As the dust settled, Pete and the stranger stood amidst the aftermath—a canyon scarred by the confrontation. The legend of the gunslinger, etched into the very rocks that bore witness, continued to echo through the borderlands. The wind, now a gentle breeze that carried the tales of the untamed West, seemed to convey a sense of justice fulfilled.

With the canyon now calm, Pete and the stranger retraced their steps, leaving the defeated Dust Devils to reckon with the consequences of their lawless pursuits. The borderlands, with its dance of shadows and stories etched into the rocky crevices, held a promise—a promise that justice, though tested by the shifting sands of time, would persist in the heart of the Wild West.

Chapter 6: Ghosts of the Ghost Town

Pistol Pete and the mysterious stranger, having quelled the storm within the borderlands, continued their journey. The sun hung low in the sky as they rode through the vast expanse, the horses' hooves creating a steady rhythm against the dusty trail. The wind, a faithful companion in the untamed West, whispered through the sagebrush, carrying tales of the journey ahead.

The trail meandered through a desolate stretch of the frontier, leading Pete and the stranger to the outskirts of a long-forgotten ghost town. Weathered buildings, their wooden structures bleached by years of exposure, stood as silent witnesses to a bygone era. The creaking of swinging doors, now rusted in place, seemed to echo through the abandoned streets.

Pete and the stranger dismounted, their boots stirring up the dust that clung to the deserted thoroughfare. The atmosphere was heavy with the weight of memories—a ghostly presence that seemed to linger among the dilapidated structures. The town, once a bustling hub of life, now stood frozen in time.

As they explored the ghost town, Pete and the stranger noticed remnants of a life interrupted. Faded signs hinted at businesses that once thrived, and shattered windows whispered tales of a past punctuated by untold struggles. The wind, carrying the melancholy of the frontier, stirred the dust in forgotten corners.

The heart of the ghost town revealed the skeletal remains of a saloon—a relic of a time when laughter and music filled its once-hallowed walls. Pete and the stranger entered cautiously, the floorboards creaking beneath their weight. The interior, bathed in a sepia-toned light filtering through the broken windows, felt like a sepulcher for memories long past.

Behind the weathered bar, bottles lined the shelves, their contents evaporated into the dry air. The silence was interrupted only by the occasional flutter of a tattered curtain or the distant call of a lone coyote. The stranger, their gaze steady, seemed to absorb the essence of the ghost town—a place where the spirits of the past coexisted with the present.

Pete, his eyes scanning the room for any signs of life, noticed a series of faded photographs on the wall. Images of families, once bound by dreams of prosperity, stared back through the sepia veil of time. Pete's thoughts drifted to his own family, the echoes of their laughter blending with the wind's mournful wail.

A sudden noise disrupted the ghostly quiet—a distant rattle, like the echoes of forgotten footsteps. Pete and the stranger exchanged glances, their instincts sharpened by the unpredictable nature of the frontier. Following the sound, they navigated the ghost town's deserted streets, the shadows of the past shifting with every step.

The noise led them to the remnants of a once-grand hotel, its faded sign bearing the name "Frontier Lodge." The door, slightly ajar, swung with a haunting creak as they entered. Inside, a flickering lantern cast long shadows on the peeling wallpaper. The air seemed charged with the presence of unseen observers.

As Pete and the stranger explored the upper floors, they stumbled upon a room that seemed frozen in time. The furniture, draped in dusty sheets, hinted at a hasty departure. A diary, its pages yellowed with age, lay open on a wooden dresser. Pete, his eyes scanning the handwritten entries, glimpsed a narrative of joy, sorrow, and the relentless march of time.

The diary told the tale of a family that once called the ghost town home—a family whose dreams were eclipsed by the shadows of the frontier. The stranger, their features still hidden beneath the wide-brimmed hat, absorbed the narrative with a quiet reverence. The ghost town, it seemed, held more than just weathered structures—it cradled the stories of lives intertwined with the unforgiving landscape.

A sudden chill filled the air as the distant rattle grew louder. Pete and the stranger, drawn by an unseen force, descended to the ghost town's outskirts. There, at the edge of the desolate streets, they discovered the source of the mysterious sound—an old piano, its keys touched by an invisible hand.

The wind, now carrying the notes of a melancholic melody, seemed to dance through the ghost town. Pete and the stranger, captivated by the spectral performance, stood in silent reverence. The piano, though weathered by time, echoed with the echoes of a bygone era—a haunting reminder of the lives that once sought solace in the heart of the frontier.

As the last notes faded into the desert breeze, the ghost town returned to its silent slumber. Pete and the stranger, moved by the ethereal experience, left the abandoned streets behind. The wind, now a gentle whisper carrying the tunes of the past, accompanied them as they rode towards the next chapter of their unfolding saga.

The sun dipped below the horizon, casting long shadows over the ghost town. The horses' hooves echoed through the empty streets as Pete and the stranger disappeared into the twilight, leaving the memories of the past to rest among the faded structures. The frontier, with its ghosts and untold tales, held more mysteries for them to unravel—a journey that stretched beyond the remnants of a forgotten town and into the heart of the boundless West.

Chapter 7: Echoes of the Mesa

Pistol Pete and the mysterious stranger rode into the vast expanse, leaving the ghost town behind. The trail led them through sprawling mesas, their towering formations reaching towards the azure sky. The sun, now descending on the horizon, cast long shadows that danced across the rugged landscape.

As they traversed the mesa's uneven terrain, Pete and the stranger felt the magnetic pull of an ancient energy—an energy that seemed to resonate with the untold tales of the land. The wind, weaving through the towering rock formations, carried with it whispers of stories etched into the stone. The horses' hooves echoed through the canyons, a symphony that harmonized with the rustling leaves and the distant calls of hidden critters.

At the base of a colossal mesa, Pete and the stranger dismounted, their eyes drawn to petroglyphs etched into the sandstone. The ancient carvings told stories of generations long past—a narrative of survival, connection, and a symbiotic dance with the untamed frontier. Pete, running his fingers over the weathered carvings, felt a connection to the spirits that lingered within the rocks.

The stranger, their gaze fixed on the mesmeric patterns, seemed to decipher the language of the petroglyphs. It was a language that spoke of challenges faced and victories won—a testament to the resilience of those who had navigated the boundless West before them. The mesa, with its silent carvings, became a portal to a time where survival meant understanding the intricate dance of nature and the relentless passage of seasons.

As the day waned, Pete and the stranger ascended the mesa, following a winding trail that snaked through the rocky outcrops. The elevation provided a panoramic view of the sprawling frontier—the undulating mesas, the patchwork of distant canyons, and the tapestry of colors painted by the setting sun. The wind, now a gentle breeze at the mesa's summit, carried with it a sense of both solitude and interconnectedness.

At the peak, Pete and the stranger found a natural alcove that offered shelter from the evening breeze. The horses, tethered nearby, grazed on the sparse vegetation that clung to the mesa's rocky surface. The stranger, their features still hidden beneath the wide-brimmed hat, seemed to commune with the ancient spirits that whispered through the canyon winds.

Around the flickering campfire, Pete and the stranger shared a simple meal—their reflections blending with the shadows cast by the dancing flames. The mesa, with its timeless energy, seemed to invite them into a communion with the land. Pete, his gaze fixed on the star-studded sky, felt a sense of humility in the face of the vast universe that stretched beyond the horizon.

As night fell over the mesa, the air filled with the haunting calls of nocturnal creatures. Pete, leaning back against the sandstone alcove, listened intently to the symphony of the night—the distant hoots of owls, the rustle of unseen critters, and the gentle hum of the wind. The stranger, still and silent, absorbed the essence of the mesa as if communing with the very spirits that had left their mark on the stone canvas.

In the quiet of the mesa's summit, Pete and the stranger took turns keeping watch over the slumbering frontier. The stars overhead seemed to blink in approval, their light filtering through the ancient petroglyphs. The mesa, with its timeless tales etched into the rock, stood as a sentinel overlooking the vast expanse.

As the night deepened, Pete and the stranger found solace in the shared silence. The wind, a gentle caress against the mesa's sandstone face, carried with it the promise of a new day. With the first light of dawn, they descended from the summit, leaving the ancient carvings to be kissed by the morning sun.

As they resumed their journey across the mesas, Pete and the stranger felt a newfound connection to the untamed West—a connection forged by the echoes of the mesa and the spirits that lingered within its rocky embrace. The wind, now a steadfast companion, carried with it the stories of the land—a land that held mysteries, challenges, and the boundless beauty of the Wild West.

The mesas, with their towering presence and silent carvings, became waypoints in the unfolding saga of Pistol Pete and the mysterious stranger. As they rode into the horizon, the wind continued to carry the echoes of the mesa—whispers of resilience, whispers of timelessness, and the eternal tales etched into the very heart of the frontier.

Chapter 8: The Crossing at Coyote Creek

Pistol Pete and the mysterious stranger, their journey through the mesas behind them, rode towards the distant horizon. The trail led them through a vast expanse dotted with sagebrush, the horses' hooves creating a rhythmic symphony against the dusty ground. The sun, a golden orb in the cloudless sky, cast a warm glow over the sprawling frontier.

As they rode, Pete and the stranger approached the banks of Coyote Creek—a winding watercourse that carved through the landscape. The sound of flowing water and the rustling leaves of cottonwood trees signaled the presence of life amidst the vastness of the frontier. The creek, its banks lined with vibrant wildflowers, seemed to beckon the weary travelers to its refreshing embrace.

Pete and the stranger, guided by the winding trail, reached the edge of Coyote Creek. The horses, sensing the proximity of water, neighed with anticipation. Pete, his eyes scanning the surroundings, noticed a weathered wooden bridge spanning the creek—a crossing worn by countless travelers before them. The stranger, draped in the tattered serape, led the way towards the bridge.

Upon reaching the creek's edge, Pete and the stranger dismounted. The horses, grateful for the respite, drank from the crystal-clear waters. The stranger, their gaze fixed on the meandering course of the creek, seemed to absorb the tranquility of the scene. The air was filled with the melody of nature—the babbling of the creek, the chirping of crickets, and the distant call of a mockingbird.

As they approached the bridge, Pete noticed weathered planks and faded paint—a testament to the countless journeys that had crossed this threshold. The bridge, though showing signs of age, stood sturdy and reliable, a silent witness to the ebb and flow of the untamed West. Pete and the stranger exchanged a glance, a silent acknowledgment of the crossing that lay ahead.

Midway across the bridge, Pete and the stranger paused. The creek flowed beneath them, its waters reflecting the azure sky. Pete, his gaze fixated on the rippling current, felt a sense of introspection—a realization that each crossing held its own significance in the vast tapestry of the frontier.

As they continued their journey, Pete and the stranger reached the other side of Coyote Creek. The landscape unfolded before them, a patchwork of rolling hills and distant canyons. The wind, carrying the scent of sagebrush and the promise of new horizons, seemed to urge them forward. The horses, refreshed from their drink, eagerly pressed on.

The trail, now leading through a series of hills, offered panoramic views of the expansive frontier. Pete and the stranger rode side by side, the mesas and canyons blending into a mosaic of earthy hues. The stranger, their eyes hidden beneath the wide-brimmed hat, spoke in sparse words of the journey and the mysteries that lay ahead.

As they ascended a hill, the landscape shifted once again. A valley unfolded before them, carpeted with golden grasses that swayed in the breeze. A herd of antelope grazed in the distance, their graceful movements adding to the serenity of the scene. Pete and the stranger, now immersed in the tranquility of the valley, allowed themselves a moment of respite.

Setting up a modest camp in the valley, Pete and the stranger gathered around a crackling fire. The warmth of the flames, a companion in the cool evening, cast flickering shadows on the valley floor. The stranger, their features illuminated by the dancing light, shared tales of the frontier—of uncharted territories, hidden oases, and the unyielding spirit of those who called the Wild West home.

As night descended over the valley, the stars painted the sky with their brilliant glow. Pete and the stranger, their silhouettes outlined against the celestial canvas, contemplated the vastness of the frontier. The valley, cradled between the hills, seemed to hold its breath as if participating in the silent conversation between the two travelers.

Under the blanket of stars, Pete and the stranger took turns keeping watch over the valley. The wind, a gentle lullaby in the quiet night, carried with it the promise of new beginnings. The frontier, with its ever-changing landscapes and unspoken tales, held a chapter yet to be written.

With the first light of dawn, Pete and the stranger broke camp and resumed their journey. The valley, now bathed in the soft hues of morning, bid farewell to the travelers as they ventured towards the next horizon. Coyote Creek, with its crossing and the serenity of the valley, became waypoints in the unfolding saga—a saga written in the language of the untamed West, where each trail, each crossing, carried the echoes of the frontier's eternal song.

Chapter 9: Shadows of the Whispering Pines

Pistol Pete and the mysterious stranger, their horses forging a path through the undulating terrain, continued their journey into the heart of the frontier. The trail led them into a dense forest of whispering pines, the towering trees casting dappled shadows on the forest floor. The air, fragrant with the scent of pine needles, held an enchanting stillness that seemed to echo with the secrets of the woods.

As they ventured deeper into the forest, the sunlight filtered through the thick canopy, creating a mosaic of light and shade. The horses, their hooves muffled by the pine needles carpeting the ground, moved with a quiet grace. Pete and the stranger, their eyes alert to the nuances of the wooded expanse, navigated the labyrinth of towering trunks and winding trails.

The stranger, draped in the tattered serape, seemed attuned to the whispers of the pines—an unseen guide through the shadows that danced beneath the branches. Pete, his senses sharpened by years in the wild, noticed the subtle shifts in the forest—a rustle in the underbrush, the distant call of a bird, and the occasional scampering of woodland creatures.

As they followed the trail, Pete and the stranger reached a clearing bathed in the soft glow of filtered sunlight. The clearing, surrounded by ancient pines, seemed to hold a timeless quality—a sanctuary within the heart of the forest. The horses, sensing the tranquility of the space, grazed contentedly on the lush grass.

In the center of the clearing stood an ancient stone well, its moss-covered surface attesting to its age. Pete, drawn to the well by an unseen force, approached and peered into its depths. The water, clear as crystal, reflected the surrounding pines and seemed to hold the secrets of the forest within its liquid embrace.

The stranger, standing alongside Pete, gestured towards the well with a subtle nod. It was as if the well, with its mysterious allure, beckoned them to listen to the whispers of the pines and the tales woven into the fabric of the forest. Pete, his hand trailing through the cool water, felt a connection to the untamed beauty that surrounded them.

As the day progressed, Pete and the stranger decided to rest in the clearing—a respite beneath the ancient pines. The horses, tethered nearby, found shade beneath the towering trees. The stranger, their features partially revealed by the dappled sunlight, shared tales of the forest —of creatures that roamed in the moonlit hours, of hidden springs that quenched the thirst of both man and beast, and of the mystical energy that permeated the wooded expanse.

In the quiet of the forest, a soft breeze stirred the pine needles overhead. The trees, their branches forming a natural canopy, whispered tales of the ancient spirits that guarded the heart of the wilderness. Pete, leaning against the rough bark of a pine, absorbed the essence of the forest—a place where time seemed to stand still, and the rustling leaves spoke in a language known only to those who listened with their hearts.

As evening descended, Pete and the stranger kindled a campfire in the clearing. The flames, dancing in the gathering dusk, cast a warm glow that pushed back the encroaching shadows. The stranger, their gaze fixed on the flickering embers, shared stories of the hidden trails that crisscrossed the forest—a network of winding paths that connected distant corners of the untamed frontier.

Under the starlit sky, Pete and the stranger marveled at the celestial display overhead. The whispering pines, their branches forming a cathedral-like ceiling, seemed to invite the travelers into a silent communion with the cosmos. The night, punctuated by the soft calls of nocturnal creatures, unfolded in a timeless dance between shadow and light.

As they slept beneath the whispering pines, Pete and the stranger dreamt of the forest's secrets—the ancient tales etched into the bark, the spirits that danced among the branches, and the ever-changing symphony of the wild. The forest, with its enigmatic allure, cradled them in its embrace, weaving their dreams into the very fabric of the untamed West.

With the first light of dawn, Pete and the stranger bid farewell to the clearing and the whispering pines. The trail, now leading them out of the forest, promised new landscapes and the mysteries yet to be unveiled. The horses, their coats dappled with the morning dew, eagerly pressed on, carrying the echoes of the forest within the hoofbeats that resonated through the boundless frontier. The shadows of the whispering pines, though left behind, lingered in the hearts of the travelers as they rode towards the next chapter of their unfolding saga.

Chapter 10: Serenade of the Silver Canyon

Pistol Pete and the mysterious stranger rode out of the whispering pines, the forest's enigmatic embrace lingering in the air as they ventured deeper into the frontier. The trail led them towards the horizon, where the landscape transitioned into a vast stretch of canyons and mesas. The sun, a radiant orb in the expansive sky, cast a warm glow over the ever-changing tableau of the Wild West.

As they rode, the terrain shifted beneath the hooves of their horses. The trail guided them towards the entrance of Silver Canyon—a majestic ravine whose walls gleamed with the silver hues of the exposed rock. The air, now filled with the scent of sagebrush and the promise of adventure, hummed with an energy unique to the canyons that crisscrossed the untamed frontier.

Pete and the stranger approached the canyon's edge, where the trail descended into its depths. The horses, sure-footed companions in the rugged landscape, carefully navigated the winding path. As they descended, the walls of Silver Canyon rose like ancient sentinels, their silver veins shimmering in the sunlight.

Midway through the descent, the canyon widened into a breathtaking vista. The trail led them to a natural amphitheater—a vast expanse surrounded by towering rock formations. The stranger, draped in the tattered serape, seemed to sense the significance of the canyon's embrace. Pete, his eyes scanning the panoramic view, felt a sense of reverence for the majesty that unfolded before them.

In the heart of Silver Canyon, the travelers decided to make camp. The horses, tethered on a flat plateau, gazed out over the expansive canyon floor. The stranger, their features partially revealed by the wide-brimmed hat, gestured towards the surrounding rock formations—a silent invitation to explore the secrets hidden within the silver-hued walls.

As the sun dipped below the canyon rim, Pete and the stranger explored the labyrinthine passages of Silver Canyon. The walls, sculpted by centuries of wind and water, seemed to tell a tale of resilience and transformation. Petroglyphs, etched into the rock by hands long gone, hinted at the lives that had once sought shelter within the canyon's embrace.

In a secluded alcove, Pete and the stranger discovered a natural spring—a crystalline pool fed by underground veins. The water, cool and refreshing, mirrored the silver hues of the canyon walls. The stranger, their eyes reflecting the colors of the rock, approached the spring with a quiet reverence. Pete, his hands cupped to drink, felt a connection to the lifeblood that flowed within the heart of Silver Canyon.

As night fell, the canyon transformed into a celestial canvas. The stars, brilliant in the absence of city lights, painted the sky with their twinkling glow. Pete and the stranger, seated on a ledge overlooking the canyon floor, marveled at the cosmic display. The wind, carrying with it the echoes of the untamed West, whispered through the rock formations as if adding its voice to the serenade of the night.

Around the campfire, the stranger shared tales of Silver Canyon—of ancient tribes that sought refuge within its walls, of the elusive wildlife that roamed its floor, and of the enduring spirit that echoed through the silver veins of the rock. Pete, his gaze fixed on the dancing flames, absorbed the stories that wove the canyon into the very fabric of the frontier.

As the fire burned low, Pete and the stranger settled into a comfortable silence. The canyon, bathed in moonlight, held a timeless allure—a place where the boundaries between earth and sky seemed to blur. The night, punctuated by the distant calls of nocturnal creatures, wrapped the travelers in its gentle embrace.

With the first light of dawn, Pete and the stranger bid farewell to Silver Canyon. The trail, now leading them out of the rock labyrinth, promised new landscapes and challenges. The horses, rested and ready, carried the echoes of the canyon within their hoofbeats as they ventured towards the next chapter of their unfolding saga.

Silver Canyon, with its silver-hued walls and ancient tales, became a waypoint in the journey of Pistol Pete and the mysterious stranger. The wind, now a steadfast companion, carried with it the serenade of the canyon—a melodic reminder of the untamed beauty that awaited them beyond the rocky embrace. As they rode towards the horizon, the whispers of Silver Canyon echoed in their hearts, blending with the symphony of the Wild West that stretched before them.

Chapter 11: Whispers in the Whirlwind

Pistol Pete and the mysterious stranger rode out of the embrace of Silver Canyon, the echoes of the silver-hued walls fading behind them as they ventured into the expanse of the untamed frontier. The trail wound through rolling hills and expansive meadows, the horses' hooves creating a rhythmic melody against the canvas of the open landscape. The sun, a golden disc in the vast sky, bathed the frontier in a warm glow.

As they rode, the terrain gradually transformed into a sweeping plain dotted with tufts of grass and patches of wildflowers. The wind, a constant companion in the Wild West, began to pick up, carrying with it the whispers of distant tales. Pete and the stranger, their eyes scanning the horizon, felt the change in the air—a prelude to the mysteries that awaited them in the heart of the frontier.

The trail led them towards a distant mesa, its silhouette rising against the expansive sky like a sentinel guarding the secrets of the land. As they approached, the wind intensified, swirling dust devils danced across the plain, creating an otherworldly spectacle. The stranger, their serape billowing in the gusts, seemed to commune with the elements—a silent acknowledgment of the untamed forces that shaped the frontier.

At the base of the mesa, the horses slowed as the trail began to ascend. Pete and the stranger climbed higher, the panoramic view unfolding before them. The mesa, a plateau of red rock, offered a commanding vantage point over the sprawling frontier. The wind, now a constant companion, carried the scent of the earth and the distant promise of adventure.

On the mesa's summit, Pete and the stranger dismounted. The land stretched in all directions—a vast tapestry of hills, canyons, and distant mesas. The stranger, their gaze fixed on the horizon, seemed to sense the presence of something beyond the visible—a force that resonated with the very essence of the untamed West. Pete, leaning against a weathered boulder, took in the expansive view, feeling the power of the land beneath his fingertips.

As the day unfolded, Pete and the stranger explored the mesa's surface. Ancient petroglyphs adorned the red rock, telling stories of the land's vibrant past. The stranger, tracing the lines with a weathered hand, seemed to decipher the language of the symbols—a narrative of the cycles of nature, the dance of celestial bodies, and the enduring spirit of those who had walked the frontier before.

In a secluded alcove, they discovered a collection of weathered bones—a relic of a time when the mesa served as a hunting ground for ancient tribes. Pete, his fingers brushing the sun-bleached remains, felt a connection to the primal forces that had shaped the land. The wind, carrying with it the whispers of bygone eras, seemed to murmur tales of survival, challenges, and the ever-changing dance of life.

As the sun dipped below the horizon, casting long shadows over the mesa, Pete and the stranger made camp. The horses grazed on the sparse vegetation, and a campfire crackled in the cool evening air. The stranger, their face partially obscured by the flickering flames, shared stories of the mesa—of forgotten rituals, celestial observations, and the symbiotic relationship between the land and its inhabitants.

Under the canopy of stars, Pete and the stranger lay on the mesa's surface, their gazes fixed on the cosmic display overhead. The wind, now a gentle breeze, carried with it the haunting calls of nocturnal creatures. The mesa, with its ancient tales and whispered secrets, became a sanctuary for contemplation—a place where the boundaries between earth and sky blurred.

As they slept beneath the celestial dome, Pete and the stranger dreamt of the whispers in the whirlwind—the unseen forces that shaped the frontier and guided their journey. The night, with its symphony of celestial bodies and ethereal calls, cradled them in its embrace.

With the first light of dawn, Pete and the stranger bid farewell to the mesa. The trail, now leading them down from the plateau, promised new landscapes and challenges. The horses, their coats gleaming in the morning sun, carried the echoes of the mesa within their hoofbeats as they ventured towards the next chapter of their unfolding saga.

The mesa, with its timeless stories etched in rock and bone, became a waypoint in the journey of Pistol Pete and the mysterious stranger. The wind, a steadfast companion, carried with it the whispers of the whirlwind—a melodic reminder of the invisible forces that shaped the Wild West. As they rode towards the next horizon, the echoes of the mesa lingered in their hearts, blending with the ongoing symphony of the untamed West that stretched before them.

Chapter 12: Dance of the Desert Spirits

Pistol Pete and the mysterious stranger rode on from the mesa, their horses weaving through the changing landscape of the untamed frontier. The trail led them into the vastness of the desert—a sea of golden sand dunes stretching as far as the eye could see. The sun, a blazing orb in the cloudless sky, painted the desert with hues of amber and gold.

As they journeyed through the shifting sands, the horses' hooves left imprints on the desert floor. The air, dry and filled with the scent of sun-baked earth, seemed to vibrate with the energy of the desert. Pete and the stranger, their faces shielded from the sun by wide-brimmed hats, pressed on into the heart of the arid expanse.

In the distance, mirages shimmered on the horizon—a play of light and heat that teased the senses. The stranger, seemingly attuned to the secrets of the desert, guided the way through the undulating dunes. Pete, squinting against the sunlight, marveled at the beauty of the seemingly endless sea of sand.

As they rode deeper into the desert, Pete and the stranger noticed a distant formation of rocks rising from the sands. The wind, now carrying with it the soft whispers of the desert spirits, seemed to guide them towards the rocky outcrop. The horses, their ears perked in anticipation, quickened their pace as if drawn by an unseen force.

Upon reaching the rocks, Pete and the stranger discovered a hidden oasis—a small pool of clear water surrounded by hardy desert vegetation. The horses, grateful for the respite, drank from the oasis. Pete and the stranger, removing their hats to feel the cool breeze, took in the oasis's unexpected beauty in the midst of the relentless desert.

In the shade of the rocks, they decided to rest. The stranger, their gaze fixed on the shimmering heat waves in the distance, seemed lost in contemplation. Pete, wiping the sweat from his brow, felt the calming energy of the oasis—a sanctuary in the midst of the harsh desert. The wind, a gentle caress against the rocks, carried with it the tales of survival and resilience written in the very sands beneath their feet.

As the day wore on, Pete and the stranger explored the rocky formation. Petroglyphs adorned the weathered surfaces—symbols and shapes etched by the hands of those who had sought refuge in the desert's embrace. The stranger, their fingers tracing the ancient carvings, seemed to decipher the language of the rocks—a narrative of endurance, adaptation, and the unbroken spirit of the desert dwellers.

In the late afternoon, the duo climbed to the top of the rocks, where a panoramic view of the desert unfolded before them. The dunes, now bathed in the warm hues of the setting sun, stretched like waves frozen in time. The stranger, standing on the rocky precipice, raised their arms as if communing with the desert spirits that danced in the fading light.

As evening descended over the desert, Pete and the stranger made camp near the oasis. The horses, now rested and content, grazed on the resilient desert plants. The stranger, draped in the tattered serape, shared stories of the desert—of nomadic tribes that navigated the shifting sands, of hidden oases that sustained life in the arid expanse, and of the timeless dance between earth and sky.

Under the canopy of stars, Pete and the stranger sat around the campfire. The desert, now bathed in the soft glow of moonlight, seemed to come alive with unseen spirits. The stranger, their voice a rhythmic cadence in the quiet night, spoke of the desert's mysteries—the mirages that deceived, the spirits that whispered in the wind, and the enduring beauty that thrived in the most unexpected corners of the arid wilderness.

As they slept beneath the starlit sky, Pete and the stranger dreamt of the dance of the desert spirits—the ethereal figures that wove tales in the sands and spoke in the language of the wind. The night, with its celestial spectacle and the haunting calls of nocturnal creatures, cradled them in its embrace.

With the first light of dawn, Pete and the stranger bid farewell to the oasis and the rocks that stood as sentinels in the desert. The trail, now leading them away from the dunes, promised new landscapes and challenges. The horses, their coats dusted with the sands of the desert, carried the echoes of the oasis within their hoofbeats as they ventured towards the next chapter of their unfolding saga.

The desert, with its silent whispers and hidden oases, became a waypoint in the journey of Pistol Pete and the mysterious stranger. The wind, now a constant companion, carried with it the tales of the desert spirits—a melodic reminder of the unseen forces that shaped the Wild West. As they rode towards the next horizon, the echoes of the desert lingered in their hearts, blending with the ongoing symphony of the untamed frontier that stretched before them.

Chapter 13: Veil of the Ghostly Canyons

Pistol Pete and the mysterious stranger rode onward, leaving the desert oasis behind as the trail wound through the ever-changing landscape of the untamed frontier. The terrain shifted once again, leading them towards the jagged outlines of distant canyons. The sun, now casting long shadows in the late afternoon, painted the rocky walls with hues of orange and red.

As they approached the canyons, Pete and the stranger noticed a peculiar quality to the landscape. The air seemed to shimmer with an ethereal light, and the distant canyons appeared almost as if veiled in a translucent curtain. The stranger, their gaze fixed on the ghostly canyons, seemed to sense the enigmatic nature of the terrain. Pete, squinting against the sun's glare, felt a sense of anticipation as they ventured deeper into the canyonlands.

The trail led them into a labyrinth of narrow passages and towering cliffs. The horses, their hooves echoing in the rocky corridors, navigated the maze with a sure-footed grace. Pete and the stranger, their eyes scanning the walls for signs of ancient stories, entered a canyon that seemed to resonate with an otherworldly energy.

As they rode deeper into the canyon, the air grew cooler, and the light took on a surreal quality. Shadows played on the rock surfaces, creating illusions that danced in the corners of Pete's vision. The stranger, riding ahead, seemed to become one with the shifting shadows, their silhouette blending with the spectral hues of the canyon.

Midway through the canyon, they discovered a natural amphitheater—a circular space surrounded by towering cliffs. In the center, a pool of water reflected the ghostly light. Pete and the stranger, drawn to the eerie beauty of the place, dismounted and approached the pool. The water, clear as crystal, seemed to hold a mirror to the mysteries concealed within the canyon's depths.

As they lingered in the amphitheater, a soft breeze whispered through the canyon, carrying with it the echoes of ghostly tales. Pete and the stranger, seated on a flat rock, felt the energy of the place—a convergence of the tangible and the intangible. The stranger, draped in the tattered serape, gestured towards the cliffs, inviting Pete to listen to the stories written in the layers of rock.

In the shifting light of dusk, Pete and the stranger made camp in the amphitheater. The horses, tethered near the pool, grazed on the sparse vegetation that clung to the canyon walls. The stranger, their eyes fixed on the star-studded sky, began to share tales of the ghostly canyons— of ancient spirits that inhabited the rocky passages, of echoes that transcended time, and of the unspoken language spoken by the wind through the canyon corridors.

Under the celestial dome, Pete and the stranger lay on their bedrolls, gazing at the stars that shimmered above the ghostly canyons. The night, silent save for the occasional rustle of the breeze, held a mystical quality. The stranger, their voice carrying the weight of ancient tales, spoke of the unseen forces that governed the canyonlands—the spirits that danced in the shadows, the phantoms that carved tales in the rock, and the timeless energy that pulsed through the very heart of the ghostly canyons.

As they slept beneath the starlit sky, Pete and the stranger dreamt of the veiled mysteries of the canyon—a realm where the boundaries between the living and the spectral blurred. The night, with its ethereal presence and the haunting calls of distant creatures, cradled them in its embrace.

With the first light of dawn, Pete and the stranger bid farewell to the ghostly canyons. The trail, now leading them out of the labyrinthine passages, promised new landscapes and challenges. The horses, their coats shimmering with the remnants of the spectral light, carried the echoes of the canyon within their hoofbeats as they ventured towards the next chapter of their unfolding saga.

The ghostly canyons, with their veiled beauty and ethereal tales, became a waypoint in the journey of Pistol Pete and the mysterious stranger. The wind, now a whispering guide, carried with it the echoes of the spectral realm—a melodic reminder of the unseen forces that shaped the Wild West. As they rode towards the next horizon, the mysteries of the ghostly canyons lingered in their hearts, blending with the ongoing symphony of the untamed frontier that stretched before them.

Chapter 14: Echoes of the Forgotten Citadel

Pistol Pete and the mysterious stranger, their journey weaving through the diverse tapestry of the untamed frontier, continued towards the next enigmatic destination. The trail led them away from the ghostly canyons, guiding them into a vast expanse of plains and hills. The sun, now hanging low in the western sky, cast a warm glow over the ever-changing landscape.

As they rode, the terrain gradually transformed into a series of low hills crowned with clusters of ancient trees. The stranger, their gaze scanning the horizon, seemed to sense a presence in the air—a subtle vibration that hinted at the proximity of something significant. Pete, his eyes attuned to the details of the frontier, followed the stranger's lead as they approached a distant rise.

At the crest of the hill, a sight unfolded before them—a forgotten citadel, its weathered walls rising against the backdrop of the setting sun. The stranger, their silhouette framed by the golden light, gestured towards the ancient structure. Pete, his curiosity piqued, urged his horse forward as they descended towards the forgotten citadel.

The citadel, surrounded by a ring of weathered stones, stood as a silent testament to a bygone era. Vines climbed the crumbling walls, and the echoes of a distant past seemed to linger in the air. Pete and the stranger, their horses treading softly over the overgrown path, approached the entrance of the citadel.

As they entered, the interior revealed a maze of corridors and chambers, each bearing the scars of time. Faded murals adorned the walls, telling tales of battles, celebrations, and the daily life of those who once inhabited the citadel. Pete, running his fingers over the ancient artwork, felt a connection to the lives that had unfolded within the forgotten walls.

In the central courtyard, a dilapidated fountain stood—a relic of a time when water flowed freely within the citadel. The stranger, their eyes reflecting the melancholy of the ruins, approached the fountain with a sense of reverence. Pete, surveying the crumbling architecture, imagined the vibrant scenes that once played out in the shadow of the citadel's towering walls.

The citadel, with its mysterious aura, seemed to invite exploration. Pete and the stranger ascended a weathered staircase that led to the highest tower. From the summit, the view stretched across the expansive frontier—the hills, the plains, and the distant canyons painted in the warm hues of the setting sun. The stranger, their gaze fixed on the horizon, seemed to commune with the echoes of a forgotten era.

As the daylight waned, Pete and the stranger decided to make camp within the citadel. The horses, tethered in the courtyard, grazed on the wild grass that pushed through the ancient stones. The stranger, draped in the tattered serape, kindled a campfire that flickered in the gathering darkness. Pete, his eyes scanning the starlit sky, felt the weight of the citadel's history—the untold stories and the enduring spirit of the forgotten realm.

Around the campfire, the stranger shared tales of the citadel—of a civilization that once thrived in harmony with the land, of the struggles that led to its eventual decline, and of the mysteries that still lingered within the crumbling walls. Pete, his gaze fixed on the dancing flames, absorbed the stories that wove the citadel into the very fabric of the untamed frontier.

Under the celestial dome, Pete and the stranger lay on their bedrolls within the citadel's courtyard. The night, silent save for the occasional rustle of leaves and the distant calls of nocturnal creatures, held a contemplative stillness. The citadel, with its ancient tales and forgotten whispers, became a sanctuary for reflection—a place where time seemed to stand still.

As they slept beneath the starlit sky, Pete and the stranger dreamt of the echoes of the forgotten citadel—the voices of those who had once walked its halls, the celebrations that had echoed through its chambers, and the resilience that had marked its slow descent into the annals of history. The night, with its ethereal presence and the haunting calls of the nocturnal creatures, cradled them in its embrace.

With the first light of dawn, Pete and the stranger bid farewell to the forgotten citadel. The trail, now leading them away from the ruins, promised new landscapes and challenges. The horses, their coats brushed by the morning dew, carried the echoes of the citadel within their hoofbeats as they ventured towards the next chapter of their unfolding saga.

The forgotten citadel, with its tales etched in stone and memory, became a waypoint in the journey of Pistol Pete and the mysterious stranger. The wind, now a gentle breeze, carried with it the echoes of the ancient realm—a melodic reminder of the enduring spirit that lingered within the forgotten walls. As they rode towards the next horizon, the mysteries of the citadel lingered in their hearts, blending with the on-going symphony of the untamed frontier that stretched before them.

Chapter 15: The Enchanted Grove

Pistol Pete and the mysterious stranger, their journey through the untamed frontier a continuous tapestry of discovery, left the forgotten citadel behind and followed the trail as it meandered through rolling hills and dense woods. The landscape transitioned into a lush expanse, filled with the vibrant colors of wildflowers and the sweet scent of blossoming trees. The sun, filtering through the thick canopy of leaves, created dappled patterns on the forest floor.

As they rode, the horses' hooves kicked up earthy fragrances, and the air became tinged with the refreshing aroma of the woods. Pete and the stranger, their senses attuned to the natural symphony around them, entered a realm untouched by time—a place that seemed to vibrate with an enchanting energy.

The trail led them deeper into the heart of the forest, where ancient trees towered overhead, their branches interwoven to create a natural cathedral of greenery. Birds, their melodies blending with the rustle of leaves, flitted from branch to branch. The stranger, their eyes reflecting the play of sunlight and shadows, seemed to recognize the enchantment woven into the grove.

Amidst the towering trees, Pete and the stranger stumbled upon a hidden glade—an open space surrounded by ancient oaks and adorned with a carpet of moss. In the center, a crystal-clear stream murmured its way through smooth stones. The horses, sensing the magic of the place, approached the stream to drink. Pete and the stranger dismounted, drawn to the serenity that enveloped the enchanted grove.

The stranger, their hand outstretched, brushed against the leaves of an ancient oak, as if greeting an old friend. Pete, his senses heightened by the mystical aura, felt a connection to the natural energy that pulsed through the grove. The air seemed to hum with life, and the vibrant colors of the wildflowers held an intensity that bordered on the otherworldly.

As they explored the grove, Pete and the stranger discovered a circle of standing stones near the stream—a hidden sanctuary within the heart of the enchanted woods. The stranger, their fingers tracing the weathered surfaces, seemed to commune with the ancient spirits that lingered in the moss-covered stones. Pete, captivated by the silent conversation, felt the presence of something beyond the tangible—the whispers of nature's guardians.

In the midst of the grove, they decided to make camp. The horses grazed on the lush grass, and a small fire crackled, casting a warm glow over the enchanting surroundings. The stranger, draped in the tattered serape, began to share tales of the enchanted grove—of a time when ancient civilizations revered the spirits of the woods, of the magic that coursed through the very veins of the land, and of the enduring bond between humanity and nature.

Under the verdant canopy, Pete and the stranger sat around the campfire. The grove, now bathed in the soft glow of moonlight filtering through the leaves, seemed to come alive with unseen spirits. The stranger, their voice a melodic cadence in the quiet night, spoke of the interconnected web of life—the dance of fireflies, the rustle of nocturnal creatures, and the ethereal beauty that thrived in the heart of the enchanted woods.

As they slept beneath the celestial canopy, Pete and the stranger dreamt of the enchantment that pulsed through the grove—the ancient spirits that whispered in the wind, the dance of moonlight on the moss-covered stones, and the timeless connection between humanity and the natural world. The night, with its magical presence and the soothing calls of nocturnal creatures, cradled them in its embrace.

With the first light of dawn, Pete and the stranger bid farewell to the enchanted grove. The trail, now leading them out of the mystical woods, promised new landscapes and challenges. The horses, their coats brushed by the morning dew, carried the echoes of the grove within their hoofbeats as they ventured towards the next chapter of their unfolding saga.

The enchanted grove, with its timeless magic and natural wonders, became a waypoint in the journey of Pistol Pete and the mysterious stranger. The wind, now a gentle whisper, carried with it the melodies of the woods—a melodic reminder of the interconnected dance of life that unfolded in the heart of the untamed frontier. As they rode towards the next horizon, the enchantment of the grove lingered in their hearts, blending with the ongoing symphony of the untamed wilderness that stretched before them.

Chapter 16: Whispers of the Twilight Mesa

Pistol Pete and the mysterious stranger, their journey carrying them through a myriad of landscapes, followed the trail as it led them towards a distant mesa bathed in the soft hues of twilight. The sun, now a crimson orb on the horizon, cast long shadows across the expansive plains. The air, cooler as the day surrendered to evening, carried with it the subtle transition between day and night.

As they approached the twilight mesa, the terrain shifted to a series of low hills, and the horses navigated their way through the undulating landscape. The stranger, their gaze fixed on the distant silhouette of the mesa, seemed to sense a unique energy emanating from the twilight-draped heights. Pete, his senses attuned to the subtle shifts in the frontier, shared a knowing glance with the stranger as they rode on.

The trail led them to the base of the mesa, where the soft glow of twilight painted the rock formations with shades of lavender and indigo. The horses, their hooves creating a rhythmic cadence against the rocky ground, carried Pete and the stranger towards the ascent. The mesa, a sentinel in the fading light, seemed to beckon them to explore its secrets.

As they climbed higher, the panorama unfolded before them. The twilight mesa offered a breathtaking view of the surrounding landscape—the rolling hills, the distant canyons, and the plains stretching towards the horizon. Pete and the stranger, their gazes captivated by the twilight-drenched tableau, felt a sense of awe at the beauty that unfolded beneath the canvas of the evening sky.

On the mesa's summit, a gentle breeze greeted them. The air, tinged with the scent of juniper and sage, seemed to carry the whispers of the twilight—a time when the boundary between day and night blurred. The stranger, their face touched by the last rays of sunlight, stood as if in communion with the evolving hues of the frontier. Pete, leaning against a weathered boulder, took in the expansive view, feeling the serenity of the mesa seep into his very being.

As the day transitioned to night, Pete and the stranger made camp on the mesa's summit. The horses, tethered nearby, grazed on the sparse vegetation that clung to the rocky surface. The stranger, their gaze fixed on the emerging stars, began to share tales of the twilight mesa—of a place where ancient tribes gathered to observe celestial events, of the spirits that roamed the mesa during the transition between light and darkness, and of the enduring connection between the land and its inhabitants.

Under the celestial dome, Pete and the stranger sat around the campfire. The mesa, now bathed in the silvery light of the moon, seemed to hold a quiet reverence for the unfolding night. The stranger, their voice a soothing cadence in the quietude, spoke of the tales etched in the mesa's stones—the cycles of celestial bodies, the ancient rituals that marked the passage of time, and the symbiotic relationship between the land and those who called it home.

As they slept beneath the starlit sky, Pete and the stranger dreamt of the whispers of the twilight mesa—the unseen forces that guided the frontier through the veil of night, the dance of shadows on the mesa's surface, and the timeless energy that pulsed through the very heart of the twilight-draped heights. The night, with its celestial ballet and the haunting calls of nocturnal creatures, cradled them in its embrace.

With the first light of dawn, Pete and the stranger bid farewell to the twilight mesa. The trail, now leading them down from the summit, promised new landscapes and challenges. The horses, their coats gleaming in the morning light, carried the echoes of the mesa within their hoofbeats as they ventured towards the next chapter of their unfolding saga.

The twilight mesa, with its serene beauty and celestial tales, became a waypoint in the journey of Pistol Pete and the mysterious stranger. The wind, now a gentle whisper, carried with it the melodies of the twilight—a melodic reminder of the seamless dance between day and night that unfolded in the untamed frontier. As they rode towards the next horizon, the whispers of the twilight mesa lingered in their hearts, blending with the ongoing symphony of the ever-changing wilderness that stretched before them.

Chapter 17: Dance of the Prairie Spirits

Pistol Pete and the mysterious stranger, their trail winding through the vast frontier, continued their journey as the landscape transitioned into expansive prairies stretching towards the distant horizon. The sun, now a golden disc in the high noon sky, painted the undulating grasslands with hues of amber and gold. The air, filled with the sweet scent of wildflowers and the distant calls of prairie birds, carried the energy of the untamed wilderness.

As they rode, the horses' hooves created a rhythmic beat against the soft earth, and the prairie winds whispered secrets that danced through the tall grass. The stranger, their eyes scanning the vastness of the plains, seemed attuned to the spirits that roamed the prairie—a realm where the untamed and the ethereal coexisted. Pete, his senses immersed in the openness of the landscape, shared a silent understanding with the stranger as they traversed the endless sea of grass.

The trail led them to a place where the prairie seemed to undulate in a natural rhythm—a vast expanse where the grasses swayed in unison with the wind. In the center, a circle of ancient stones marked a sacred space on the prairie canvas. The horses, sensing the sanctity of the place, approached the stone circle with a quiet reverence. Pete and the stranger dismounted, drawn to the energy that pulsed within the prairie dance floor.

In the midst of the stone circle, Pete and the stranger felt the heartbeat of the prairie—the pulse of the land that had witnessed countless seasons and the cyclical dance of life. The stranger, their movements mirroring the sway of the grasses, seemed to become one with the prairie spirits. Pete, his boots sinking into the soft earth, embraced the primal connection to the untamed wilderness.

As they stood in the sacred circle, the wind carried with it the haunting calls of distant creatures—the unseen inhabitants of the prairie. The stranger, their hands outstretched, gestured towards the horizon, inviting Pete to witness the dance of the prairie spirits. The grasses, now caught in an invisible choreography, moved with a grace that seemed to transcend the physical realm.

In the heart of the prairie dance floor, Pete and the stranger decided to make camp. The horses, content in the sacred space, grazed on the lush grasses. The stranger, draped in the tattered serape, kindled a campfire that crackled in the evening air. Pete, sitting on a weathered stone, felt the presence of the prairie spirits—a force that wove through the very fabric of the untamed landscape.

Around the campfire, the stranger shared tales of the prairie spirits —of ancient legends that spoke of the guardians of the grasslands, of the ethereal dances that unfolded under the vast sky, and of the timeless energy that connected the inhabitants of the prairie to the land itself. Pete, his gaze fixed on the flames, absorbed the stories that painted a vivid picture of the untamed spirits that breathed life into the prairie.

Under the starlit sky, Pete and the stranger lay on their bedrolls within the stone circle. The night, with its celestial spectacle and the haunting calls of nocturnal creatures, held a sense of communion with the prairie spirits. The stranger, their voice a melodic whisper in the quietude, spoke of the unseen forces that guided the prairie dance—the spirits that reveled in the moonlight, the echoes that resonated through the grasses, and the enduring connection between humanity and the untamed wilderness.

As they slept beneath the celestial dome, Pete and the stranger dreamt of the dance of the prairie spirits—the ethereal figures that wove tales in the grass, the rhythms that pulsed through the very heart of the plains, and the timeless energy that connected all living things on the prairie. The night, with its ethereal presence and the soothing calls of distant creatures, cradled them in its embrace.

With the first light of dawn, Pete and the stranger bid farewell to the prairie dance floor. The trail, now leading them away from the stone circle, promised new landscapes and challenges. The horses, their coats brushed by the morning dew, carried the echoes of the prairie spirits within their hoofbeats as they ventured towards the next chapter of their unfolding saga.

The prairie dance floor, with its timeless rhythms and untamed spirits, became a waypoint in the journey of Pistol Pete and the mysterious stranger. The wind, now a gentle breeze, carried with it the melodies of the prairie—a melodic reminder of the harmonious dance that unfolded under the expansive sky. As they rode towards the next horizon, the echoes of the prairie spirits lingered in their hearts, blending with the ongoing symphony of the ever-changing wilderness that stretched before them.

Chapter 18: Shadows of the Mesquite Grove

Pistol Pete and the mysterious stranger, their journey through the vast frontier an ever-unfolding saga, found themselves guided by the trail into a mesquite grove as the sun dipped below the western horizon. The air, warm with the remnants of the day, carried the sweet fragrance of mesquite blossoms. The horses, their hooves stirring the soft earth, navigated the shadowy pathways of the grove with an innate familiarity.

The stranger, their eyes attuned to the shifting patterns of light and shade, led Pete into the heart of the mesquite grove. The tall, gnarled trees cast elongated shadows on the ground, creating a dance of darkness and moonlit patches. Pete, his senses alive to the subtle nuances of the frontier, felt a mystical aura enveloping the grove—an energy that seemed to linger within the interwoven branches.

As they ventured deeper, the mesquite grove revealed hidden clearings adorned with silvery moonlight. The stranger, their silhouette blending with the shadows, moved with an ethereal grace as they explored the labyrinthine pathways. Pete, his boots crunching softly on the dry earth, marveled at the enchanting beauty that unfolded beneath the mesquite canopy.

In the heart of the grove, they discovered a natural amphitheater—a circular space surrounded by ancient mesquite trees. The stranger, their hand tracing the rough bark of one of the trees, seemed to commune with the spirits that resided within the grove. Pete, his eyes scanning the shadowy alcoves, felt a sense of reverence for the untamed energy that pulsed through the mesquite grove.

The horses, sensing the sacredness of the place, grazed on the sparse grasses within the amphitheater. Pete and the stranger, seated on a fallen log, observed the dance of shadows and moonlight that played out on the mesquite branches. The stranger, draped in the tattered serape, began to share tales of the mesquite grove—of a place where spirits found solace in the cool shadows, where echoes whispered through the rustling leaves, and where the moonlit nights held a special kind of magic.

Under the celestial canopy, Pete and the stranger decided to make camp within the mesquite grove. The horses, tethered near the clearing, became companions in the quietude of the night. The stranger, their voice carrying the weight of ancient tales, spoke of the mesquite spirits —of the guardians that watched over the grove, of the ethereal dance that unfolded under the moonlit sky, and of the timeless connection between the land and those who traversed its shadows.

Around the campfire, the mesquite grove seemed to come alive with unseen energies. The stranger's stories painted vivid pictures of the spirits that called the grove home—the whispers that carried messages on the night breeze, the shadows that danced in the moonlight, and the ancient tales etched in the very roots of the mesquite trees. Pete, his gaze fixed on the flickering flames, absorbed the stories that resonated with the mystical heart of the grove.

As they slept beneath the starlit sky, Pete and the stranger dreamt of the shadows of the mesquite grove—the spirits that moved through the moonlit branches, the ancient rhythms that echoed within the clearing, and the timeless energy that connected all living things in the heart of the frontier. The night, with its ethereal presence and the haunting calls of distant creatures, cradled them in its embrace.

With the first light of dawn, Pete and the stranger bid farewell to the mesquite grove. The trail, now leading them out of the labyrinthine pathways, promised new landscapes and challenges. The horses, their coats brushed by the morning dew, carried the echoes of the mesquite spirits within their hoofbeats as they ventured towards the next chapter of their unfolding saga.

The mesquite grove, with its shadowy beauty and ancient spirits, became a waypoint in the journey of Pistol Pete and the mysterious stranger. The wind, now a gentle whisper, carried with it the melodies of the grove—a melodic reminder of the timeless dance between light and shadow that unfolded in the untamed frontier. As they rode towards the next horizon, the shadows of the mesquite grove lingered in their hearts, blending with the ongoing symphony of the ever-changing wilderness that stretched before them.

Chapter 19: Veins of the Silver Canyon

Pistol Pete and the mysterious stranger, their trail leading them through the intricate tapestry of the frontier, embarked on a new leg of their journey that wound into the heart of the Silver Canyon. The sun, now climbing the eastern sky, cast its warm rays over the rugged terrain. The air, tinged with the scent of sagebrush and anticipation, carried with it the promise of untold tales hidden within the canyon's walls.

As they approached the entrance of the Silver Canyon, the trail transformed into a narrow passageway flanked by towering cliffs. The horses, sure-footed in the rocky terrain, navigated the winding path with a steady determination. The stranger, their gaze scanning the intricate patterns in the canyon walls, seemed to sense the ancient secrets etched into the very stones of the canyon. Pete, his eyes tracing the contours of the rugged landscape, shared a silent acknowledgment with the stranger as they ventured deeper into the Silver Canyon.

The canyon walls, made of silver-hued stone, seemed to gleam with a natural brilliance as they rose majestically on either side. The path beneath their hooves, worn smooth by centuries of travelers, led Pete and the stranger further into the depths of the canyon. The trail, carved by the persistent force of water over eons, spoke of the timeless journey that had shaped the very essence of the Silver Canyon.

As they progressed, the canyon widened, revealing a network of side passages and hidden alcoves. Pete and the stranger, guided by an unspoken understanding, explored the intricate veins of the Silver Canyon —the twists and turns that beckoned them to uncover the mysteries concealed within the heart of the rugged landscape.

In one of the canyon's alcoves, they discovered a natural spring—a crystalline pool fed by underground veins of water. The horses, their coats reflecting the silver hues of the canyon walls, drank from the refreshing pool. Pete and the stranger, their thirst quenched by the pure water, felt a connection to the lifeblood that flowed through the very veins of the Silver Canyon.

Further along the trail, the canyon walls seemed to close in, creating a narrow passage known as the Silver Gorge. The horses, their hooves echoing against the canyon walls, carried Pete and the stranger through the shadowy embrace of the gorge. The stranger, their eyes scanning the rugged terrain, guided the way with a quiet confidence. Pete, leaning into the curves of the canyon, marveled at the natural architecture that surrounded them.

As they emerged from the Silver Gorge, the canyon widened once again, revealing a sprawling basin bathed in sunlight. The Silver Canyon, with its veins of silver-hued stone and hidden alcoves, held a sense of reverence for the forces that had sculpted its timeless beauty. Pete and the stranger, their senses heightened by the grandeur of the canyon, felt a connection to the enduring spirit that flowed through the very veins of the untamed wilderness.

In the heart of the Silver Canyon, Pete and the stranger decided to make camp. The horses, tethered in a sheltered alcove, grazed on the sparse vegetation that clung to the canyon floor. The stranger, draped in the tattered serape, kindled a campfire that flickered in the evening light. Pete, sitting on a flat rock, absorbed the tranquil ambiance of the canyon—the whispers of the wind, the rustle of leaves, and the distant calls of canyon-dwelling creatures.

Around the campfire, the stranger shared tales of the Silver Canyon —of the veins of silver that had drawn prospectors in search of fortune, of the ancient ceremonies held within its hidden alcoves, and of the enduring spirit that flowed through the very heart of the rugged landscape. Pete, his gaze fixed on the dancing flames, absorbed the stories that painted a vivid picture of the untamed forces that had shaped the Silver Canyon through the ages.

As they slept beneath the starlit sky, Pete and the stranger dreamt of the veins of the Silver Canyon—the ancient currents that pulsed through the very stones, the echoes of footsteps that had traversed the winding paths, and the timeless energy that connected all living things in the heart of the rugged landscape. The night, with its celestial brilliance and the haunting calls of nocturnal creatures, cradled them in its embrace.

With the first light of dawn, Pete and the stranger bid farewell to the Silver Canyon. The trail, now leading them out of the basin, promised new landscapes and challenges. The horses, their coats shimmering in the morning sun, carried the echoes of the canyon within their hoofbeats as they ventured towards the next chapter of their unfolding saga.

The Silver Canyon, with its veins of silver-hued stone and hidden alcoves, became a waypoint in the journey of Pistol Pete and the mysterious stranger. The wind, now a gentle breeze, carried with it the melodies of the canyon—a melodic reminder of the enduring spirit that flowed through the very veins of the untamed frontier. As they rode towards the next horizon, the veins of the Silver Canyon lingered in their hearts, blending with the ongoing symphony of the ever-changing wilderness that stretched before them.

Chapter 20: Whispers of the Mystic Oasis

Pistol Pete and the mysterious stranger, their journey through the untamed frontier a kaleidoscope of landscapes, found themselves drawn towards the Mystic Oasis—a legendary sanctuary nestled amidst the sprawling wilderness. The sun, now ascending the azure sky, cast its golden rays over the landscape. The air, tinged with the fragrance of wildflowers and the anticipation of discovery, carried with it the promise of the mystical haven that awaited them.

As they approached the entrance to the Mystic Oasis, the trail led them through a series of lush meadows adorned with vibrant blooms. The horses, their hooves creating a soft melody against the earth, carried Pete and the stranger into a realm where the boundaries between reality and enchantment seemed to blur. The stranger, their eyes reflecting the awe-inspiring beauty around them, led Pete towards the heart of the oasis with a quiet assurance.

The meadows gave way to a dense thicket, and as they passed through, the air became cooler, filled with the refreshing scent of a hidden spring. Emerging from the thicket, Pete and the stranger beheld the Mystic Oasis—an emerald jewel cradled within the embrace of ancient trees. A natural pool, fed by crystal-clear waters, sparkled in the dappled sunlight. Exotic flowers adorned the edges, their colors reflecting the vibrancy of the untamed wilderness.

The stranger, their gaze fixed on the oasis, seemed to commune with the unseen forces that guarded the sacred waters. Pete, his senses attuned to the mystical aura, felt a profound connection to the oasis—a haven where the magic of the frontier revealed itself in all its splendor.

As they approached the pool, the horses, sensing the sanctity of the oasis, drank from the clear waters. Pete and the stranger, drawn to the tranquility of the place, dipped their hands into the pool, feeling the cool embrace of the mystic waters. The oasis, with its timeless beauty, held an air of serenity that seemed to transcend the hurried pace of the outside world.

In the heart of the Mystic Oasis, they discovered a natural stone platform surrounded by weeping willows. The stranger, their fingers tracing the patterns on the ancient stones, invited Pete to join them in a moment of reflection. The horses, now resting in the shade, added to the harmonious atmosphere with their occasional neighs and contented grazing.

The stranger, draped in the tattered serape, began to share tales of the Mystic Oasis—of a place where weary travelers found respite, of the spirits that guarded the sacred waters, and of the mystical rituals held under the canopy of ancient trees. Pete, his eyes fixed on the tranquil pool, absorbed the stories that painted a vivid picture of the timeless magic that pervaded the oasis.

As the day unfolded into evening, Pete and the stranger decided to make camp within the Mystic Oasis. The horses, content in the peaceful surroundings, found their own spots to rest. The stranger, kindling a campfire with wood gathered from the outskirts of the oasis, cast a warm glow over the scene. Pete, sitting on a moss-covered rock, felt the mystic energies of the oasis enveloping him—a comforting embrace that seemed to harmonize with the very essence of the untamed frontier.

Around the campfire, the stranger shared tales of the mystical rituals held within the Mystic Oasis—the dances that honored the spirits, the whispers that carried messages on the evening breeze, and the timeless connection between those who sought solace and the enchanted waters. Pete, his gaze fixed on the flickering flames, absorbed the stories that resonated with the ancient rhythms of the oasis.

As they slept beneath the celestial dome, Pete and the stranger dreamt of the whispers of the Mystic Oasis—the unseen forces that moved through the rustling leaves, the reflections that danced on the surface of the pool, and the timeless energy that connected all living things in the heart of the enchanted sanctuary. The night, with its celestial brilliance and the soothing calls of nocturnal creatures, cradled them in its embrace.

With the first light of dawn, Pete and the stranger bid farewell to the Mystic Oasis. The trail, now leading them away from the sacred waters, promised new landscapes and challenges. The horses, their coats glistening in the morning light, carried the echoes of the oasis within their hoofbeats as they ventured towards the next chapter of their unfolding saga.

The Mystic Oasis, with its emerald waters and ancient stones, became a waypoint in the journey of Pistol Pete and the mysterious stranger. The wind, now a gentle breeze, carried with it the melodies of the oasis—a melodic reminder of the timeless magic that flowed through the very heart of the untamed frontier. As they rode towards the next horizon, the whispers of the Mystic Oasis lingered in their hearts, blending with the ongoing symphony of the ever-changing wilderness that stretched before them.